About Math Connection:

SO-BBF-253

Welcome to RBP Books' Connection series. Math Connection provides students with focused practice to help reinforce and develop math skills in all areas defined by the NCTM (National Council of Teachers of Mathematics) as appropriate for fifth-grade students. These include three- and four-digit addition and subtraction, probability, measurement, geometry, graphing, fractions, time, money values, word problems, multiplication, division, and decimals. Exercises are grade-level appropriate with clear examples and instructions on each page to guide the lesson; they also feature a variety of activities to help students develop their ability to work with numbers.

© Rainbow Bridge Publishing 2003

Dear Parents and Educators,

Thank you for choosing this Rainbow Bridge Publishing educational product to help teach your children and students. We take great pride and pleasure in becoming involved with your educational experience. Some people say that math will always be math and reading will always be reading, but we do not share that opinion. Reading, math, spelling, writing, geography, science, history and all other subjects will always be some of life's most fulfilling adventures and should be taught with passion both at home and in the classroom. Because of this, we at Rainbow Bridge Publishing associate the greatness of learning with every product we create.

It is our mission to provide materials that not only explain, but also amaze; not only review, but also encourage; not only guide, but also lead. Every product contains clear, concise instructions, appropriate sample work and engaging, grade-appropriate content created by classroom teachers and writers that is based on national standards to support your best educational efforts. We hope you enjoy our company's products as you embark on your adventure. Thank you for bringing us along.

Sincerely,

George Starks
Associate Publisher
Rainbow Bridge Publishing

Math Connection™ • Grade 5
Written by Brenda Gardner

© 2003 Rainbow Bridge Publishing. All rights reserved.

Permission to Reproduce

Rainbow Bridge Publishing grants the right to the individual purchaser to reproduce the student activity materials in this book for noncommercial individual or classroom use only. Reproduction for an entire school or school system is strictly prohibited. No part of this publication may be reproduced for storage in a retrieval system or transmitted in any form or by any means, electronic, mechanical, recording, or otherwise, without the prior written permission of the publisher.
For information, call or write: Rainbow Bridge Publishing, Inc. • PO Box 571470 • Salt Lake City, Utah 84157-1470 • Tel: (801) 268-8887

Illustrations
Amanda Sorensen

Visual Design and Layout
Andy Carlson, Robyn Funk, Zachary Johnson, Scott Whimpey

Publisher
Scott G. Van Leeuwen

Editorial Director
Paul Rawlins

Associate Publisher
George Starks

Copy Editors and Proofreaders
Kim Carlson, Elaine Clark, Lauren Mauery, Linda Swain

Series Creator
Michele Van Leeuwen

Technology Integration
James Morris, Dante J. Orazzi

Please visit our website at
www.summerbridgeactivities.com
for supplements, additions, and corrections to this book.

First Edition 2003

For orders call 1-800-598-1441
Discounts available for quantity orders

ISBN: 1-932210-17-2

PRINTED IN THE UNITED STATES OF AMERICA
10 9 8 7 6 5 4 3 2 1

Math Connection – Grade 5
Table of Contents

Tips for Learning Multiplication Facts

The most common way to learn multiplication facts is memorization. This method requires plenty of practice. Since not all students learn the same way, it may help some students to memorize multiplication facts through visual and/or auditory (listening) senses.

Tips:

1. Make flashcards. Have your child make a card for each multiplication fact that he or she needs to memorize. Be sure to include all numbers (i.e., write a card for 2 x 3 and a different card for 3 x 2). Write the answers on the back. Encourage your child to use these cards at home, in the car, or anytime you have some extra time.

   Here's a variation: Use the answer side of your flashcard and come up with as many multiplication problems as you can. For example: If the number (answer) is 12, you can come up with 3 x 4, 4 x 3, 2 x 6, 6 x 2, 1 x 12, and 12 x 1. Practicing this way will help prepare you for division as well.

2. Work with one set at a time until your child is comfortable with the set. Don't always go in order. Have your child say the answers out loud. Start by working with the 2's (2 x 1 = 2, 2 x 2 = 4, 2 x 3, 2 x 4, 2 x 5, etc.). Once your child is comfortable, reverse the order (1 x 2, 2 x 2, 3 x 2, 4 x 2, 5 x 2, etc.) and again practice until answers come immediately. Have your child memorize the "easier" sets (1's, 2's, 5's, 4's, and 9's) before moving on to the "harder" sets (3's, 7's, 8's).

3. Here are some hints to help with certain sets:
   a. For the 2's, just double the number, or add the number to itself.
   b. For the 5's, the answer must end in 5 or 0.
   c. For the 4's. Double the number and then double again.
      i. For example, if you are multiplying 4 x 7, double 7 to get 14, and then double 14 to get 28.
   d. For the 9's, use your fingers. Hold out all 10 fingers. Put down the finger that is being multiplied by 9. Your answer is the digits that are left before and after the finger that is down.
      i. For example, if you are multiplying 9 x 7, count over 7 fingers. Tuck the seventh finger down. You'll have **6 fingers and 3 fingers, to make 63.**

  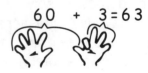

   ii. Another hint for 9's' is that the digits in the answer must add up to 9.

4. Don't give the answer to your child. Instead, show them how to find the answer. Draw a rectangle using numbers being multiplied as the lengths of the sides, or help your child think about multiples or adding the number the number of needed times.

5. Be creative. Take a break if you need to. Try a different strategy. Have your child make up a rhyme or silly story to help them remember a multiplication fact that is giving them trouble. Most of all, encourage your child and be patient.

© RBP Books   www.summerbridgeactivities.com   **Math Connection—Grade 5—RBP0172**

Problem-Solving Strategies

Here are a few strategies to help improve problem solving.

1. Read through the entire problem.
2. Find what the problem is asking for. You may have to re-read the problem. Underline what you are trying to find or write it in your own words.
3. Decide how to solve the problem.
   a. Will you need to add, subtract, multiply, or divide to find the answer?
   b. Will you need to do more than one operation?
   c. Will you need to use some other strategy?
   d. Visualize the situation.
   e. Find a pattern, make a table, guess and check, work backwards, or draw a picture.
   f. Know the common key words found in problem stories:

Key words	Operation
sum, total, add	addition
difference, subtract, less	subtraction
product, multiply	multiplication
quotient, divide	division

Problem Solving Strategies

Draw a Diagram
Use Logical Reasoning
Look for a Pattern
Guess and Check
Use Objects/Act It Out
Make an Organized List
Make a Table
Solve a Simpler Problem
Work Backward

4. Solve the problem.
5. Check your answer.

Example: Eliza has 14 apples and 32 oranges. How many more oranges than apples does she have? How many fruits does she have altogether?

1. Read through the problem
2. What is the problem asking for?
   In this problem we want to find two things. First, we need to find how many more apples than oranges there are. Second, we need to know the total number of fruits.
3. Decide how to solve the problem.
   We have two questions, so we need two answers.
   a. To find how many more oranges Eliza has, we will need to subtract.
   b. To find the total number of fruits, we will need to add.
4. Solve the problem.
   a. Subtract 32 − 14. The answer is 18. So there are 18 more oranges.
   b. Add 14 + 32 = 46 total fruits.
5. Check your answer(s).
   a. If there are 18 oranges left, then 18 + the number of apples should equal 32 oranges.
      So, is 18 + 14 = 32? Yes.
   b. If there are 46 fruits, then 46 minus the oranges should equal the apples. 46 − 32 = 14 apples. This checks.

We love this math stuff!

Math Connection—Grade 5—RBP0172   www.summerbridgeactivities.com   ©RBP Books

Pre-Test: Addition and Subtraction

Add or subtract.

Keep your eyes open for those tricky signs!

1.
43	63	60	55	92
+ 41	+ 49	+ 11	+ 24	+ 25

2.
308	429	154	785	126
+ 769	+ 578	+ 842	+ 732	+ 579

3.
1,249	9,753	36,553	99,373	511,060
+ 8,764	+ 7,893	+ 92,834	+ 192,752	+ 846,456

4.
32	214	213	5,453	83,246
79	566	384	1,628	76,483
+ 30	+ 800	+ 543	+ 8,453	+ 17,758

5.
150	5,449	6,616	24,622	29,502
130	3,908	5,431	76,556	7,574
76	5,680	4,045	1,154	33,762
+ 97	+ 5,615	5,483	9,903	93,041
		+ 2,944	+ 46,147	+ 23,429

6.
24	65	53	468	578
− 12	− 38	− 49	− 54	− 38

7.
535	980	859	8,756	5,890
− 526	− 578	− 589	− 4,895	− 4,895

8.
5,890	6,789	9,835	57,897	67,893
− 3,948	− 5,789	− 5,780	− 5,893	− 57,893

15

Addition
Add

1. 1   5   8   9   3   4   2   6
    + 6   + 5   + 1   + 6   + 9   + 7   + 4   + 8

2. 4   4   9   3   9   2   6   6
    + 6   + 1   + 4   + 5   + 2   + 2   + 3   + 2

3. 5   7   9   7   6   7   2   8
    + 6   + 7   + 9   + 5   + 7   + 1   + 3   + 8

4. 7   2   0   1   9   6   3   6
    + 8   + 5   + 2   + 7   + 0   + 4   + 7   + 1

5. 8   4   2   4   6   6   9   8
    + 3   + 4   + 9   + 5   + 6   + 5   + 7   + 5

6. 4   3   2   1   5   3   8   1
    + 8   + 8   + 7   + 3   + 1   + 2   + 2   + 2

7. 8   7   3   8   9   3   6   8
    + 6   + 6   + 6   + 7   + 1   + 1   + 0   + 9

8. 1   7   4   9   7   3   5   2
    + 4   + 9   + 3   + 3   + 2   + 4   + 2   + 6

9. 5   1   8   1   9   5   0   7
    + 4   + 2   + 0   + 9   + 5   + 3   + 6   + 4

10. 7   2   5   2   5   4   8   4
    + 3   + 3   + 7   + 1   + 9   + 9   + 4   + 2

www.summerbridgeactivities.com   ©RBP Books

Addition

Add columns right to left.

Ok, smile and say "3-digit addition!"

347	Add the **ones**.	
+ 656	Carry the **ten** to	
13	the tens column.	

1		
347	Add the **tens**.	
+ 656	Carry the **hundred** to	
103	the hundreds column.	

1	
347	Add the **hundreds**
+ 656	column.
1,003	

1.
```
  295        620        681        496        723
+ 610      + 274      + 143      + 674      + 213
```

2.
```
  829        713        863        648        173
+ 469      + 847      + 140      + 810      + 726
```

3.
```
  199        480        518        915        249
+ 314      + 393      + 622      + 409      + 217
```

4.
```
  483        571        266        174        276
+ 195      + 861      + 510      + 717      + 755
```

5.
```
  163        399        994        946        870
+ 375      + 196      + 176      + 693      + 519
```

6.
```
  216        805        153        691        119
+ 929      + 933      + 386      + 690      + 266
```

7.
```
  101        517        601        160        238
+ 928      + 348      + 516      + 993      + 998
```

8.
```
  555        166        107        177        446
+ 891      + 103      + 718      + 358      + 818
```

© RBP Books www.summerbridgeactivities.com Math Connection—Grade 5—RBP0172

Addition
Add columns right to left.

$\begin{array}{r} 1 \\ 2{,}537 \\ +\ 4{,}724 \\ \hline 1 \end{array}$	$\begin{array}{r} 1 \\ 2{,}537 \\ +\ 4{,}724 \\ \hline 61 \end{array}$	$\begin{array}{r} 1\ \ 1 \\ 2{,}537 \\ +\ 4{,}724 \\ \hline 261 \end{array}$	$\begin{array}{r} 1\ \ 1 \\ 2{,}537 \\ +\ 4{,}724 \\ \hline \mathbf{7{,}261} \end{array}$

1.
$\begin{array}{r} 4{,}510 \\ +\ 4{,}689 \\ \hline \end{array}$
$\begin{array}{r} 7{,}166 \\ +\ 5{,}622 \\ \hline \end{array}$
$\begin{array}{r} 2{,}198 \\ +\ 2{,}516 \\ \hline \end{array}$
$\begin{array}{r} 6{,}043 \\ +\ 6{,}428 \\ \hline \end{array}$
$\begin{array}{r} 4{,}025 \\ +\ 1{,}298 \\ \hline \end{array}$

2.
$\begin{array}{r} 1{,}889 \\ +\ 8{,}458 \\ \hline \end{array}$
$\begin{array}{r} 7{,}168 \\ +\ 2{,}362 \\ \hline \end{array}$
$\begin{array}{r} 5{,}530 \\ +\ 9{,}022 \\ \hline \end{array}$
$\begin{array}{r} 6{,}046 \\ +\ 5{,}539 \\ \hline \end{array}$
$\begin{array}{r} 2{,}270 \\ +\ 8{,}696 \\ \hline \end{array}$

3.
$\begin{array}{r} 8{,}979 \\ +\ 3{,}285 \\ \hline \end{array}$
$\begin{array}{r} 5{,}328 \\ +\ 5{,}991 \\ \hline \end{array}$
$\begin{array}{r} 6{,}135 \\ +\ 1{,}170 \\ \hline \end{array}$
$\begin{array}{r} 2{,}030 \\ +\ 6{,}537 \\ \hline \end{array}$
$\begin{array}{r} 1{,}947 \\ +\ 1{,}835 \\ \hline \end{array}$

4.
$\begin{array}{r} 7{,}564 \\ +\ 5{,}167 \\ \hline \end{array}$
$\begin{array}{r} 3{,}504 \\ +\ 1{,}606 \\ \hline \end{array}$
$\begin{array}{r} 3{,}044 \\ +\ 4{,}492 \\ \hline \end{array}$
$\begin{array}{r} 5{,}013 \\ +\ 8{,}362 \\ \hline \end{array}$
$\begin{array}{r} 3{,}501 \\ +\ 4{,}530 \\ \hline \end{array}$

5.
$\begin{array}{r} 2{,}044 \\ +\ 5{,}367 \\ \hline \end{array}$
$\begin{array}{r} 9{,}600 \\ +\ 8{,}664 \\ \hline \end{array}$
$\begin{array}{r} 7{,}187 \\ +\ 3{,}436 \\ \hline \end{array}$
$\begin{array}{r} 2{,}385 \\ +\ 5{,}652 \\ \hline \end{array}$
$\begin{array}{r} 3{,}643 \\ +\ 7{,}244 \\ \hline \end{array}$

6.
$\begin{array}{r} 28{,}734 \\ +\ 60{,}828 \\ \hline \end{array}$
$\begin{array}{r} 55{,}877 \\ +\ 66{,}244 \\ \hline \end{array}$
$\begin{array}{r} 46{,}780 \\ +\ 46{,}687 \\ \hline \end{array}$
$\begin{array}{r} 65{,}464 \\ +\ 98{,}795 \\ \hline \end{array}$
$\begin{array}{r} 24{,}336 \\ +\ 55{,}051 \\ \hline \end{array}$

7.
$\begin{array}{r} 26{,}634 \\ +\ 24{,}997 \\ \hline \end{array}$
$\begin{array}{r} 75{,}019 \\ +\ 82{,}226 \\ \hline \end{array}$
$\begin{array}{r} 66{,}777 \\ +\ 19{,}607 \\ \hline \end{array}$
$\begin{array}{r} 44{,}041 \\ +\ 17{,}092 \\ \hline \end{array}$
$\begin{array}{r} 70{,}292 \\ +\ 40{,}323 \\ \hline \end{array}$

8.
$\begin{array}{r} 28{,}436 \\ +\ 40{,}700 \\ \hline \end{array}$
$\begin{array}{r} 11{,}929 \\ +\ 86{,}552 \\ \hline \end{array}$
$\begin{array}{r} 61{,}649 \\ +\ 34{,}566 \\ \hline \end{array}$
$\begin{array}{r} 82{,}175 \\ +\ 58{,}026 \\ \hline \end{array}$
$\begin{array}{r} 6{,}390 \\ +\ 69{,}918 \\ \hline \end{array}$

Addition

Add.

Add columns right to left.

Add the ones. Then continue to add columns right to left.

```
          12 1 2
2,758 →  8      2,758
17,268 → 8     17,268
20,820 → 0     20,820
+ 52,314 → 4  + 52,314
          20   93,160
```

1.

430	754	174	427	786
978	904	370	140	442
+ 557	+ 723	+ 254	+ 222	+ 209

2.

4,210	012	5,816	6,318	2,477
9,733	923	1,116	8,833	4,841
+ 1,358	+ 7 25	+ 6,676	+ 7,381	+ 5,713

3.

136	7,16	419	2,342	54,331
435	2,300	6,304	49,534	23,097
257	4,671	2,783	14,735	24,781
+ 375	+ 9,610	+ 8,901	+ 58,651	+ 25,672

4.

253	475	2,742	4,432	4,825
430	234	7,463	9,857	43,029
249	987	4,687	1,248	12,064
475	178	2,115	7,824	16,753
+ 958	+ 572	+ 2,950	+ 5,432	+ 58,439

5.

476	546	1,564	15,761	4,567
578	4,789	457	27,892	18,796
483	4,871	5 793	489,741	124
473	1,753	6 82	156,474	34,897
571	154	34, 4	152,767	123
+ 128	+ 1,674	+ 3,4	+ 8,243	+ 4,576

© RBP Books   www.summerbridgeactivities.com   **Math Connection—Grade 5—RBP0172**

Subtraction

Subtract.

1.
$$\begin{array}{r}5\\-4\\\hline\end{array}\qquad\begin{array}{r}8\\-2\\\hline\end{array}\qquad\begin{array}{r}8\\-3\\\hline\end{array}\qquad\begin{array}{r}4\\-2\\\hline\end{array}\qquad\begin{array}{r}5\\-3\\\hline\end{array}\qquad\begin{array}{r}9\\-7\\\hline\end{array}\qquad\begin{array}{r}9\\-2\\\hline\end{array}\qquad\begin{array}{r}8\\-6\\\hline\end{array}$$

2.
$$\begin{array}{r}7\\-2\\\hline\end{array}\qquad\begin{array}{r}3\\-2\\\hline\end{array}\qquad\begin{array}{r}6\\-2\\\hline\end{array}\qquad\begin{array}{r}4\\-1\\\hline\end{array}\qquad\begin{array}{r}2\\-1\\\hline\end{array}\qquad\begin{array}{r}9\\-8\\\hline\end{array}\qquad\begin{array}{r}8\\-4\\\hline\end{array}\qquad\begin{array}{r}6\\-5\\\hline\end{array}$$

3.
$$\begin{array}{r}7\\-6\\\hline\end{array}\qquad\begin{array}{r}8\\-7\\\hline\end{array}\qquad\begin{array}{r}7\\-4\\\hline\end{array}\qquad\begin{array}{r}6\\-1\\\hline\end{array}\qquad\begin{array}{r}4\\-3\\\hline\end{array}\qquad\begin{array}{r}7\\-1\\\hline\end{array}\qquad\begin{array}{r}5\\-2\\\hline\end{array}\qquad\begin{array}{r}9\\-1\\\hline\end{array}$$

4.
$$\begin{array}{r}5\\-0\\\hline\end{array}\qquad\begin{array}{r}4\\-0\\\hline\end{array}\qquad\begin{array}{r}5\\-1\\\hline\end{array}\qquad\begin{array}{r}8\\-5\\\hline\end{array}\qquad\begin{array}{r}9\\-3\\\hline\end{array}\qquad\begin{array}{r}8\\-1\\\hline\end{array}\qquad\begin{array}{r}6\\-4\\\hline\end{array}\qquad\begin{array}{r}7\\-3\\\hline\end{array}$$

5.
$$\begin{array}{r}6\\-3\\\hline\end{array}\qquad\begin{array}{r}3\\-1\\\hline\end{array}\qquad\begin{array}{r}9\\-5\\\hline\end{array}\qquad\begin{array}{r}7\\-5\\\hline\end{array}\qquad\begin{array}{r}14\\-6\\\hline\end{array}\qquad\begin{array}{r}16\\-7\\\hline\end{array}\qquad\begin{array}{r}12\\-5\\\hline\end{array}\qquad\begin{array}{r}11\\-3\\\hline\end{array}$$

6.
$$\begin{array}{r}13\\-6\\\hline\end{array}\qquad\begin{array}{r}18\\-9\\\hline\end{array}\qquad\begin{array}{r}17\\-9\\\hline\end{array}\qquad\begin{array}{r}15\\-7\\\hline\end{array}\qquad\begin{array}{r}12\\-3\\\hline\end{array}\qquad\begin{array}{r}9\\-4\\\hline\end{array}\qquad\begin{array}{r}11\\-2\\\hline\end{array}\qquad\begin{array}{r}10\\-4\\\hline\end{array}$$

7.
$$\begin{array}{r}10\\-3\\\hline\end{array}\qquad\begin{array}{r}14\\-8\\\hline\end{array}\qquad\begin{array}{r}9\\-6\\\hline\end{array}\qquad\begin{array}{r}17\\-8\\\hline\end{array}\qquad\begin{array}{r}12\\-9\\\hline\end{array}\qquad\begin{array}{r}5\\-5\\\hline\end{array}\qquad\begin{array}{r}15\\-9\\\hline\end{array}\qquad\begin{array}{r}10\\-7\\\hline\end{array}$$

8.
$$\begin{array}{r}15\\-6\\\hline\end{array}\qquad\begin{array}{r}13\\-5\\\hline\end{array}\qquad\begin{array}{r}8\\-8\\\hline\end{array}\qquad\begin{array}{r}16\\-8\\\hline\end{array}\qquad\begin{array}{r}1\\-1\\\hline\end{array}\qquad\begin{array}{r}10\\-5\\\hline\end{array}\qquad\begin{array}{r}15\\-8\\\hline\end{array}\qquad\begin{array}{r}6\\-6\\\hline\end{array}$$

Math Connection—Grade 5—RBP0172   www.summerbridgeactivities.com   © RBP Books

Subtraction

Subtract. Check your answers.

Subtract columns right to left.			Check:
27 − 16 **1**	Subtract the **ones**.	27 − 16 11	Subtract the **tens**.	11 + 16 27

1.
```
  79        34        93        47
- 13      - 20      - 51      - 23
```

2.
```
  76        23        70        88
- 35      - 10      - 30      - 27
```

3.
```
  47        76        99        57
- 17      - 52      - 70      - 17
```

4.
```
  29        91        41        79
- 27      - 81      - 11      - 55
```

5.
```
  75        45        72        43
- 53      - 21      - 21      - 11
```

6.
```
  84        47        92        68
- 12      - 16      - 71      - 33
```

7.
```
  97        66        94        27
- 63      - 12      - 81      - 12
```

©RBP Books   www.summerbridgeactivities.com   Math Connection—Grade 5—RBP0172

Subtraction

Subtract. Check your answers.

OK folks, let's hear it for 2-digit subtraction!

Subtract columns right to left.	Subtract	Check:
73 – 18	Since we can't subtract 8 from 3, borrow 10 from the tens column.	6 1 X3 – 18 **55**	55 + 18 73

1.
```
  60        94        41        93
– 59      – 26      – 14      – 56
```

2.
```
  81        54        72        76
– 70      – 29      – 43      – 27
```

3.
```
  85        31        91        51
– 80      – 25      – 18      – 25
```

4.
```
  78        43        90        61
– 33      – 24      – 44      – 53
```

5.
```
  92        91        70        62
– 45      – 89      – 18      – 18
```

6.
```
  62        91        61        82
– 26      – 82      – 53      – 73
```

7.
```
  72        50        75        81
– 29      – 23      – 66      – 39
```

Math Connection—Grade 5—RBP0172   www.summerbridgeactivities.com   © RBP Books

Subtraction

Subtract.

	Subtract columns right to left.				
	652 − 484	Borrow from the tens. Subtract.	⁴¹ 6̸5̸2 − 484 **8**	Borrow from the hundreds. Subtract.	⁵ ¹⁴¹ 6̸5̸2 − 484 **68**	Subtract the hundreds.	⁵ ¹⁴¹ 6̸5̸2 − 484 **168**

1.
    738   442   818   965   752   898
    − 264   − 190   − 147   − 466   − 734   − 897

2.
    993   933   749   953   234   757
    − 295   − 848   − 247   − 539   − 105   − 206

3.
    893   914   231   757   805   895
    − 647   − 325   − 158   − 743   − 804   − 872

4.
    632   932   904   618   757   916
    − 247   − 802   − 114   − 339   − 375   − 791

5.
    795   999   836   159   160   299
    − 673   − 998   − 468   − 144   − 106   − 113

6.
    889   728   608   928   502   863
    − 141   − 654   − 376   − 581   − 278   − 776

7.
    481   686   829   578   904   509
    − 328   − 189   − 593   − 268   − 393   − 260

© RBP Books   www.summerbridgeactivities.com   Math Connection—Grade 5—RBP0172

Subtraction

Subtract.

Subtract columns right to left.		Borrow from the tens. Continue to borrow as needed to subtract.	$7^{1}1^{1}2\ 1$ 58,235 $-\ 7,786$ **50,449**
58,235 $-\ 7,786$			

1.
3,186	7,964	6,522	5,885	6,733
$-\ 2,123$	$-\ 1,280$	$-\ 4,910$	$-\ 5,347$	$-\ 5,942$

2.
9,901	9,483	8,436	6,625	5,167
$-\ 4,576$	$-\ 7,376$	$-\ 4,987$	$-\ 1,784$	$-\ 1,170$

3.
85,350	87,401	81,761	97,342	68,797
$-\ 4,383$	$-\ 9,289$	$-\ \ \ 815$	$-\ 5,052$	$-\ 8,749$

4.
60,721	66,595	74,118	33,688	97,810
$-\ 9,485$	$-\ 4,684$	$-\ 3,982$	$-\ 1,962$	$-\ 5,219$

5.
90,646	75,460	46,054	16,470	84,192
$-\ 86,247$	$-\ 16,933$	$-\ 13,241$	$-\ 14,549$	$-\ 39,559$

6.
99,543	79,583	25,911	51,313	99,564
$-\ 54,109$	$-\ 58,149$	$-\ 20,300$	$-\ 46,851$	$-\ 98,300$

Math Connection—Grade 5—RBP0172 www.summerbridgeactivities.com ©RBP Books

Problem Solving

 Football Game Attendance

Game 1	Game 2	Game 3	Game 4	Game 5
1,248	985	879	1,163	2,472

1. How many total seats were filled during the first and second games?

2. How many more people attended the first game than the second?

3. What was the total attendance for all 5 football games?

4. How many more people attended the 5 games than an estimated 5000?

5. What was the difference between the highest-attended game and the lowest-attended game?

© RBP Books   www.summerbridgeactivities.com   Math Connection—Grade 5—RBP0172

Problem Solving

1. Mrs. Johnson's fifth grade class has a goal of reading a total of 2,000 books in four weeks. If the students read 926 books in two weeks, how many more books do they need to read to reach their goal?

2. During the next two weeks, the class read an additional 1,205 books. How many total books have they read?

3. How many more books did they read than their goal of 2,000?

4. Mr. Monson's classroom decided to beat Mrs. Johnson's goal. They made a goal to read 3,000 books in four weeks. They read 1,075 books in two weeks. How many more books do they need to read to reach their goal of 3,000?

5. In the next two weeks, the class read an additional 1,643 books. How many total books did Mr. Monson's class read?

6. Did they meet their goal?

Post-Test: Addition and Subtraction

1.
```
    35        47        56        74        17
  + 48      + 84      + 37      + 28      + 84
```

2.
```
   348       748       578       273       578
 + 387     + 272     + 192     + 758     + 905
```

3.
```
  1,284     5,785    57,832    90,474   262,752
+ 3,894   + 2,489   + 5,983  + 57,825 + 187,293
```

4.
```
    43       483       548     2,478    84,710
    58       578       526     5,891    57,892
  + 34     + 901     + 102   + 5,789  + 56,982
```

5.
```
    12        23       457     4,893    58,903
    57       589     4,789     1,029     2,890
    92       901     9,074    47,892     5,890
   + 4      + 47   + 5,781  + 57,891  + 90,125
```

6.
```
    53        78        81       686       672
  - 47      - 56      - 65     - 531     - 498
```

7.
```
   428       904     5,783     7,928     5,789
 - 382     - 487     - 378   - 5,783   - 2,891
```

8.
```
 57,891    89,241    57,891    78,924   890,247
- 2,782   - 4,823  - 18,472  - 57,812 - 378,218
```

© RBP Books   www.summerbridgeactivities.com   Math Connection—Grade 5—RBP0172

Problem Solving with Money

Mr. Harper's store sells the following items.

Item	Cost
Shirt	$19
Jeans	$26
Package of Socks	$5
Shoes	$38
Jacket	$54

1. Jose wants to buy a shirt and pair of jeans from Mr Harper's store. How much money does he need?

2. If Josh buys one package of socks and a pair of shoes, how much money will he need?

3. Joseph needs a whole new wardrobe. He plans on buying all five items (shirt, jeans, socks, shoes, and jacket). He has $100.
   a. What is the total dollar amount of all of the items he wants to purchase?

   b. How much money does he still need?

4. What is the difference between the cost of a jacket and a pair of shoes?

5. If Joe has $25, and he only wants one of each item, what is the most he can purchase?

6. Jose returns the shirt that he purchased and decides to buy a jacket instead. How much more money will he need to pay?

Pre-Test: Multiplication

Multiply.

1.
3	5	15	72
x 7	x 6	x 9	x 8

2.
415	859	25	78
x 5	x 6	x 57	x 19

3.
523	689	678	159
x 38	x 57	x 80	x 91

4.
342	583	782	238
x 421	x 902	x 718	x 890

5.
4,892	5,783	6,782	1,328
x 578	x 712	x 871	x 947

© RBP Books   www.summerbridgeactivities.com   Math Connection—Grade 5—RBP0172

Multiplication

Multiply.

1. $\begin{array}{r} 8 \\ \times\,2 \\ \hline \end{array}$ $\begin{array}{r} 6 \\ \times\,5 \\ \hline \end{array}$ $\begin{array}{r} 0 \\ \times\,5 \\ \hline \end{array}$ $\begin{array}{r} 9 \\ \times\,7 \\ \hline \end{array}$ $\begin{array}{r} 2 \\ \times\,9 \\ \hline \end{array}$ $\begin{array}{r} 8 \\ \times\,4 \\ \hline \end{array}$ $\begin{array}{r} 3 \\ \times\,3 \\ \hline \end{array}$ $\begin{array}{r} 4 \\ \times\,6 \\ \hline \end{array}$

2. $\begin{array}{r} 1 \\ \times\,8 \\ \hline \end{array}$ $\begin{array}{r} 7 \\ \times\,2 \\ \hline \end{array}$ $\begin{array}{r} 1 \\ \times\,1 \\ \hline \end{array}$ $\begin{array}{r} 4 \\ \times\,0 \\ \hline \end{array}$ $\begin{array}{r} 6 \\ \times\,1 \\ \hline \end{array}$ $\begin{array}{r} 2 \\ \times\,3 \\ \hline \end{array}$ $\begin{array}{r} 2 \\ \times\,5 \\ \hline \end{array}$ $\begin{array}{r} 9 \\ \times\,4 \\ \hline \end{array}$

3. $\begin{array}{r} 6 \\ \times\,7 \\ \hline \end{array}$ $\begin{array}{r} 2 \\ \times\,1 \\ \hline \end{array}$ $\begin{array}{r} 7 \\ \times\,1 \\ \hline \end{array}$ $\begin{array}{r} 0 \\ \times\,7 \\ \hline \end{array}$ $\begin{array}{r} 4 \\ \times\,7 \\ \hline \end{array}$ $\begin{array}{r} 2 \\ \times\,6 \\ \hline \end{array}$ $\begin{array}{r} 7 \\ \times\,5 \\ \hline \end{array}$ $\begin{array}{r} 9 \\ \times\,5 \\ \hline \end{array}$

4. $\begin{array}{r} 1 \\ \times\,3 \\ \hline \end{array}$ $\begin{array}{r} 6 \\ \times\,5 \\ \hline \end{array}$ $\begin{array}{r} 1 \\ \times\,8 \\ \hline \end{array}$ $\begin{array}{r} 6 \\ \times\,9 \\ \hline \end{array}$ $\begin{array}{r} 2 \\ \times\,7 \\ \hline \end{array}$ $\begin{array}{r} 5 \\ \times\,2 \\ \hline \end{array}$ $\begin{array}{r} 5 \\ \times\,4 \\ \hline \end{array}$ $\begin{array}{r} 9 \\ \times\,2 \\ \hline \end{array}$

5. $\begin{array}{r} 7 \\ \times\,4 \\ \hline \end{array}$ $\begin{array}{r} 8 \\ \times\,3 \\ \hline \end{array}$ $\begin{array}{r} 7 \\ \times\,8 \\ \hline \end{array}$ $\begin{array}{r} 4 \\ \times\,4 \\ \hline \end{array}$ $\begin{array}{r} 9 \\ \times\,1 \\ \hline \end{array}$ $\begin{array}{r} 2 \\ \times\,1 \\ \hline \end{array}$ $\begin{array}{r} 9 \\ \times\,5 \\ \hline \end{array}$ $\begin{array}{r} 6 \\ \times\,7 \\ \hline \end{array}$

6. $\begin{array}{r} 3 \\ \times\,6 \\ \hline \end{array}$ $\begin{array}{r} 7 \\ \times\,8 \\ \hline \end{array}$ $\begin{array}{r} 6 \\ \times\,4 \\ \hline \end{array}$ $\begin{array}{r} 6 \\ \times\,6 \\ \hline \end{array}$ $\begin{array}{r} 1 \\ \times\,5 \\ \hline \end{array}$ $\begin{array}{r} 0 \\ \times\,8 \\ \hline \end{array}$ $\begin{array}{r} 8 \\ \times\,4 \\ \hline \end{array}$ $\begin{array}{r} 7 \\ \times\,6 \\ \hline \end{array}$

7. $\begin{array}{r} 7 \\ \times\,3 \\ \hline \end{array}$ $\begin{array}{r} 8 \\ \times\,3 \\ \hline \end{array}$ $\begin{array}{r} 8 \\ \times\,9 \\ \hline \end{array}$ $\begin{array}{r} 3 \\ \times\,9 \\ \hline \end{array}$ $\begin{array}{r} 9 \\ \times\,1 \\ \hline \end{array}$ $\begin{array}{r} 5 \\ \times\,8 \\ \hline \end{array}$ $\begin{array}{r} 7 \\ \times\,5 \\ \hline \end{array}$ $\begin{array}{r} 4 \\ \times\,3 \\ \hline \end{array}$

8. $\begin{array}{r} 8 \\ \times\,5 \\ \hline \end{array}$ $\begin{array}{r} 9 \\ \times\,1 \\ \hline \end{array}$ $\begin{array}{r} 3 \\ \times\,4 \\ \hline \end{array}$ $\begin{array}{r} 8 \\ \times\,9 \\ \hline \end{array}$ $\begin{array}{r} 4 \\ \times\,8 \\ \hline \end{array}$ $\begin{array}{r} 2 \\ \times\,4 \\ \hline \end{array}$ $\begin{array}{r} 2 \\ \times\,8 \\ \hline \end{array}$ $\begin{array}{r} 8 \\ \times\,3 \\ \hline \end{array}$

9. $\begin{array}{r} 8 \\ \times\,6 \\ \hline \end{array}$ $\begin{array}{r} 1 \\ \times\,9 \\ \hline \end{array}$ $\begin{array}{r} 9 \\ \times\,0 \\ \hline \end{array}$ $\begin{array}{r} 4 \\ \times\,3 \\ \hline \end{array}$ $\begin{array}{r} 9 \\ \times\,5 \\ \hline \end{array}$ $\begin{array}{r} 5 \\ \times\,4 \\ \hline \end{array}$ $\begin{array}{r} 8 \\ \times\,9 \\ \hline \end{array}$ $\begin{array}{r} 2 \\ \times\,6 \\ \hline \end{array}$

10. $\begin{array}{r} 7 \\ \times\,7 \\ \hline \end{array}$ $\begin{array}{r} 3 \\ \times\,5 \\ \hline \end{array}$ $\begin{array}{r} 4 \\ \times\,1 \\ \hline \end{array}$ $\begin{array}{r} 8 \\ \times\,1 \\ \hline \end{array}$ $\begin{array}{r} 4 \\ \times\,7 \\ \hline \end{array}$ $\begin{array}{r} 7 \\ \times\,2 \\ \hline \end{array}$ $\begin{array}{r} 9 \\ \times\,3 \\ \hline \end{array}$ $\begin{array}{r} 0 \\ \times\,6 \\ \hline \end{array}$

Math Connection—Grade 5—RBP0172   www.summerbridgeactivities.com   ©RBP Books

Multiplication

Multiply.

	56	Multiply the ones. 56	Carry the **4** to the tens column.	4 56	Multiply the tens. Add the **4**. 4 56	4 56
	x 7	x 7		x 7	x 7	x 7
		42		2		392

1.
  27 42 49 95 74 78
  x 6 x 5 x 7 x 1 x 2 x 8

2.
  31 90 34 37 20 18
  x 4 x 9 x 2 x 1 x 9 x 7

3.
  12 34 37 13 25 73
  x 5 x 8 x 9 x 2 x 5 x 7

4.
  24 11 64 36 49 43
  x 6 x 0 x 5 x 9 x 1 x 4

5.
  54 63 62 68 54 70
  x 2 x 0 x 3 x 2 x 6 x 11

6.
  87 33 61 72 87 10
  x 7 x 0 x 8 x 6 x 4 x 1

7.
  84 92 45 31 90 69
  x 6 x 9 x 5 x 4 x 7 x 2

8.
  50 23 41 77 51 88
  x 5 x 1 x 2 x 3 x 2 x 0

© RBP Books
www.summerbridgeactivities.com

Math Connection—Grade 5—RBP0172

Multiplication

Multiply.

785 $\times\ 3$	$\mathbf{785}$ $\times\ \mathbf{3}$ $\mathbf{15}$	Put the 5 in the ones place in the answer. Carry the **1** to the tens column.	$\overset{1}{785}$ $\times\ 3$ 5	Multiply the tens. Add the **1**.	785 $+\ 3$ 255	Put the 5 in the tens place in the answer. Carry the **2** to the hundreds column. Multiply 7×3, then add **2**.	$\overset{21}{785}$ $\times\ 3$ $\mathbf{2,355}$

1.
$$174 \times 2 \qquad 649 \times 1 \qquad 914 \times 6 \qquad 863 \times 5 \qquad 717 \times 2 \qquad 308 \times 8$$

2.
$$632 \times 4 \qquad 998 \times 3 \qquad 373 \times 9 \qquad 974 \times 3 \qquad 875 \times 7 \qquad 505 \times 8$$

3.
$$269 \times 6 \qquad 499 \times 4 \qquad 450 \times 8 \qquad 424 \times 5 \qquad 279 \times 7 \qquad 401 \times 3$$

4.
$$408 \times 6 \qquad 859 \times 2 \qquad 964 \times 4 \qquad 510 \times 9 \qquad 772 \times 1 \qquad 396 \times 4$$

5.
$$698 \times 7 \qquad 774 \times 3 \qquad 239 \times 5 \qquad 383 \times 2 \qquad 353 \times 9 \qquad 458 \times 0$$

6.
$$414 \times 4 \qquad 279 \times 2 \qquad 951 \times 7 \qquad 137 \times 9 \qquad 708 \times 4 \qquad 330 \times 5$$

7.
$$338 \times 1 \qquad 877 \times 6 \qquad 196 \times 3 \qquad 515 \times 9 \qquad 508 \times 5 \qquad 171 \times 1$$

Math Connection—Grade 5—RBP0172   www.summerbridgeactivities.com   ©RBP Books

Multiplication

Multiply.

| 1. | 451 | 891 | 924 | 403 | 860 | 178 |
| | x 7 | x 3 | x 2 | x 6 | x 8 | x 5 |

| 2. | 871 | 519 | 830 | 534 | 131 | 480 |
| | x 1 | x 9 | x 6 | x 2 | x 8 | x 3 |

| 3. | 494 | 138 | 983 | 551 | 843 | 248 |
| | x 7 | x 6 | x 9 | x 1 | x 4 | x 3 |

| 4. | 554 | 399 | 103 | 948 | 152 | 218 |
| | x 4 | x 5 | x 2 | x 7 | x 4 | x 6 |

| 5. | 690 | 492 | 889 | 845 | 141 | 467 |
| | x 5 | x 8 | x 9 | x 6 | x 4 | x 1 |

| 6. | 223 | 465 | 750 | 459 | 682 | 293 |
| | x 5 | x 4 | x 1 | x 8 | x 2 | x 9 |

| 7. | 818 | 120 | 343 | 344 | 346 | 285 |
| | x 5 | x 8 | x 9 | x 8 | x 6 | x 4 |

| 8. | 817 | 252 | 979 | 539 | 365 | 376 |
| | x 5 | x 2 | x 7 | x 9 | x 4 | x 4 |

| 9. | 361 | 323 | 934 | 207 | 182 | 441 |
| | x 5 | x 7 | x 3 | x 4 | x 9 | x 0 |

©RBP Books   www.summerbridgeactivities.com   Math Connection—Grade 5—RBP0172

Multiplication
Multiply.

		Multiply the ones. (69 x 5)	Multiply the tens. (69 x 30)	Add.
	69 x 35	4 69 x 35 345	2 69 x 35 345 2,070	69 x 35 345 + 2,070 2,415

1.
79	33	25	69	42	29
x 78	x 34	x 67	x 94	x 70	x 62

2.
45	88	23	96	57	58
x 47	x 20	x 43	x 23	x 38	x 99

3.
35	32	92	69	45	26
x 94	x 97	x 55	x 51	x 99	x 61

4.
66	73	11	98	32	40
x 48	x 18	x 94	x 50	x 41	x 55

5.
19	18	99	78	51	57
x 29	x 69	x 20	x 94	x 94	x 33

6.
50	35	73	14	97	70
x 75	x 27	x 63	x 55	x 98	x 86

Multiplication

Multiply.

1. 549   893   441   753
     x 901   x 828   x 170   x 139

2. 313   345   207   116
     x 674   x 962   x 323   x 201

3. 2,432   6,085   4,118   8,651
     x 406   x 485   x 739   x 134

4. 2,633   2,575   2,496   8,999
     x 242   x 383   x 964   x 396

5. 6,793   9,054   1,710   4,036
     x 152   x 885   x 365   x 478

© RBP Books www.summerbridgeactivities.com   Math Connection—Grade 5—RBP0172

Mixed Multiplication

Multiply.

1.
$$\begin{array}{r} 8 \\ \times\,7 \\ \hline \end{array}$$
$$\begin{array}{r} 10 \\ \times\,2 \\ \hline \end{array}$$
$$\begin{array}{r} 36 \\ \times\,5 \\ \hline \end{array}$$
$$\begin{array}{r} 94 \\ \times\,4 \\ \hline \end{array}$$

2.
$$\begin{array}{r} 139 \\ \times\,0 \\ \hline \end{array}$$
$$\begin{array}{r} 455 \\ \times\,2 \\ \hline \end{array}$$
$$\begin{array}{r} 378 \\ \times\,8 \\ \hline \end{array}$$
$$\begin{array}{r} 862 \\ \times\,5 \\ \hline \end{array}$$

3.
$$\begin{array}{r} 19 \\ \times\,16 \\ \hline \end{array}$$
$$\begin{array}{r} 45 \\ \times\,12 \\ \hline \end{array}$$
$$\begin{array}{r} 18 \\ \times\,62 \\ \hline \end{array}$$
$$\begin{array}{r} 83 \\ \times\,37 \\ \hline \end{array}$$

4.
$$\begin{array}{r} 75 \\ \times\,30 \\ \hline \end{array}$$
$$\begin{array}{r} 62 \\ \times\,45 \\ \hline \end{array}$$
$$\begin{array}{r} 13 \\ \times\,93 \\ \hline \end{array}$$
$$\begin{array}{r} 28 \\ \times\,43 \\ \hline \end{array}$$

5.
$$\begin{array}{r} 316 \\ \times\,916 \\ \hline \end{array}$$
$$\begin{array}{r} 387 \\ \times\,286 \\ \hline \end{array}$$
$$\begin{array}{r} 688 \\ \times\,450 \\ \hline \end{array}$$
$$\begin{array}{r} 651 \\ \times\,313 \\ \hline \end{array}$$

6.
$$\begin{array}{r} 4{,}935 \\ \times\,550 \\ \hline \end{array}$$
$$\begin{array}{r} 7{,}282 \\ \times\,243 \\ \hline \end{array}$$
$$\begin{array}{r} 9{,}771 \\ \times\,608 \\ \hline \end{array}$$
$$\begin{array}{r} 9{,}914 \\ \times\,194 \\ \hline \end{array}$$

Math Connection—Grade 5—RBP0172   www.summerbridgeactivities.com   © RBP Books

Problem Solving

Columbia Elementary is doing a fund-raiser to buy new computers for their classrooms. They plan on selling dinner tickets to their parents and neighbors. Each of the classes has been assigned to help out in purchasing the needed items. The local grocery store is advertising the following specials:

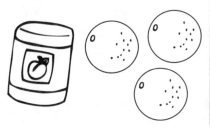

Item	Cost
Oranges	$1 per pound
Can of Fruit	$2 each
Chicken	$5 a package
Nuts	$7 per pound
Steak	$6 per pound

1. Mrs. Browning has volunteered to make a fruit salad for the school fund-raiser. She needs to buy 12 cans of fruit. How much will the 12 cans of fruit cost her?

2. Mrs. Browning also needs to buy oranges. She figures that she will need to purchase 22 pounds of oranges. How much will she have to spend on oranges?

3. Mrs. Browning's recipe calls for two pounds of nuts. She plans on doubling the recipe.
   a. How many pounds of nuts will she need?

   b. How much will it cost her?

4. Mr. Willits is in charge of buying chicken. He figures that he needs to buy 65 packages in order to feed everyone. How much will he have to spend on chicken?

5. Mr. Willits is also planning on purchasing steak for those who don't want chicken. He plans on having to buy 31 pounds of steak. How much money will he need to spend on steak?

6. Mr. Willits's class can serve 15 people in one minute. How many people can they serve in 45 minutes?

©RBP Books   www.summerbridgeactivities.com   Math Connection—Grade 5—RBP0172

Problem Solving

Mrs. Harmer's class has made a goal to complete a total of 1,000 hours of service in their community during the school year.

1. Randy decided to volunteer at a nursing home. He spent 2 hours a week helping the senior citizens. He volunteered for 23 weeks. How many hours did he volunteer at the nursing home?

2. Ruth spent 5 hours each Saturday for 15 weeks cleaning up the trash on Main Street. How many hours did she volunteer?

3. Thirteen students decided to volunteer at the food bank twice a week for 2 hours. They volunteered for 17 weeks. How many total hours did the thirteen students put in?

4. Four students worked at the homeless shelter preparing and serving food. They each volunteered for 53 hours. How many hours did the 4 students put in altogether?

5. If there were 19 students in the class (each mentioned in the previous problems).
   a. How many total hours did they volunteer?

   b. Did they meet their goal? (Hint: Add your previous answers.)

Math Connection—Grade 5—RBP0172   www.summerbridgeactivities.com   ©RBP Books

Post-Test: Multiplication

Multiply.

1.
$$\begin{array}{r} 5 \\ \times 9 \\ \hline \end{array}$$
$$\begin{array}{r} 3 \\ \times 7 \\ \hline \end{array}$$
$$\begin{array}{r} 43 \\ \times 8 \\ \hline \end{array}$$
$$\begin{array}{r} 76 \\ \times 4 \\ \hline \end{array}$$

2.
$$\begin{array}{r} 234 \\ \times 8 \\ \hline \end{array}$$
$$\begin{array}{r} 679 \\ \times 7 \\ \hline \end{array}$$
$$\begin{array}{r} 47 \\ \times 46 \\ \hline \end{array}$$
$$\begin{array}{r} 28 \\ \times 10 \\ \hline \end{array}$$

3.
$$\begin{array}{r} 534 \\ \times 87 \\ \hline \end{array}$$
$$\begin{array}{r} 461 \\ \times 49 \\ \hline \end{array}$$
$$\begin{array}{r} 478 \\ \times 82 \\ \hline \end{array}$$
$$\begin{array}{r} 572 \\ \times 34 \\ \hline \end{array}$$

4.
$$\begin{array}{r} 236 \\ \times 743 \\ \hline \end{array}$$
$$\begin{array}{r} 578 \\ \times 392 \\ \hline \end{array}$$
$$\begin{array}{r} 832 \\ \times 920 \\ \hline \end{array}$$
$$\begin{array}{r} 924 \\ \times 127 \\ \hline \end{array}$$

5.
$$\begin{array}{r} 4{,}593 \\ \times 507 \\ \hline \end{array}$$
$$\begin{array}{r} 7{,}923 \\ \times 783 \\ \hline \end{array}$$
$$\begin{array}{r} 4{,}893 \\ \times 489 \\ \hline \end{array}$$
$$\begin{array}{r} 6{,}781 \\ \times 248 \\ \hline \end{array}$$

© RBP Books   www.summerbridgeactivities.com   Math Connection—Grade 5—RBP0172

Number Patterns

Find the next number in the patterns below.

1. 4, 8, 16, 32, 64, _____

2. 1, 4, 7, 10, 13, 16, _____

3. 3, 5, 8, 12, 17, 23, _____

4. 6, 36, 66, 96, _____

5. 1, 4, 7, 6, 9, 12, 11, _____

6. 3, 3, 6, 5, 5, 10, 8, 8, 16, 13, 13, _____

7. 1, 2, 2, 3, 4, 5, 5, 6, 7, 8, 8, 9, 10, _____

8. 1, 1, 1, 3, 2, 2, 2, 6, 5, 5, 5, 15, 14, 14, 14, _____

I'm before Allie!

I'm between!

I'm after Allie!

Math Connection—Grade 5—RBP0172   www.summerbridgeactivities.com   ©RBP Books

Pre-Test: Division

Divide.

1. $3\overline{)72}$ $8\overline{)44}$ $6\overline{)472}$ $5\overline{)346}$

2. $4\overline{)2{,}408}$ $2\overline{)1{,}240}$ $16\overline{)67}$ $17\overline{)74}$

3. $31\overline{)91}$ $26\overline{)89}$ $34\overline{)120}$ $82\overline{)783}$

4. $24\overline{)560}$ $45\overline{)361}$ $92\overline{)3{,}457}$ $57\overline{)5{,}712}$

5. $15\overline{)1{,}475}$ $81\overline{)8{,}138}$ $21\overline{)39{,}464}$ $49\overline{)31{,}092}$

© RBP Books   www.summerbridgeactivities.com   **Math Connection—Grade 5—RBP0172**

Division
Divide.

 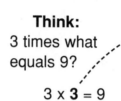

$3\overline{)9}$

Think:
3 times what
equals 9?

$3 \times \mathbf{3} = 9$

$\begin{array}{r} \mathbf{3} \\ 3\overline{)9} \\ -\ 9 \\ \hline 0 \end{array}$ Subtract.

1. $8\overline{)56}$ $6\overline{)54}$ $8\overline{)32}$ $4\overline{)12}$ $2\overline{)2}$ $3\overline{)6}$

2. $2\overline{)4}$ $7\overline{)21}$ $7\overline{)49}$ $9\overline{)81}$ $4\overline{)24}$ $8\overline{)24}$

3. $5\overline{)45}$ $5\overline{)30}$ $7\overline{)28}$ $9\overline{)72}$ $3\overline{)3}$ $6\overline{)30}$

4. $7\overline{)63}$ $9\overline{)0}$ $1\overline{)8}$ $1\overline{)4}$ $8\overline{)64}$ $5\overline{)10}$

5. $3\overline{)6}$ $3\overline{)21}$ $6\overline{)0}$ $9\overline{)18}$ $2\overline{)14}$ $6\overline{)6}$

6. $8\overline{)40}$ $8\overline{)16}$ $2\overline{)0}$ $9\overline{)9}$ $5\overline{)35}$ $6\overline{)12}$

Math Connection—Grade 5—RBP0172   www.summerbridgeactivities.com   © RBP Books

Division
Divide.

Place 2 in the tens column to represent 20. ↓

$$3\overline{)78}$$

Think: 3 times what number is closest to, but is less than or equal to, 78?

$$\begin{array}{r} 2 \\ 3\overline{)78} \\ -60 \\ \hline 18 \end{array}$$

3 x 10 = 30 Too small
3 x **20** = 60
3 x 30 = 90 Too big

Think: 3 times what number is closest to, but is less than or equal to, 18?

$$\begin{array}{r} 26 \\ 3\overline{)78} \\ -60 \\ \hline 18 \\ -18 \\ \hline 0 \end{array}$$

3 x **6** = 18

1. $1\overline{)16}$ $8\overline{)96}$ $4\overline{)92}$ $5\overline{)95}$ $3\overline{)99}$

2. $3\overline{)57}$ $1\overline{)11}$ $2\overline{)36}$ $6\overline{)72}$ $6\overline{)84}$

3. $7\overline{)91}$ $9\overline{)72}$ $3\overline{)87}$ $2\overline{)60}$ $4\overline{)84}$

4. $6\overline{)90}$ $9\overline{)54}$ $3\overline{)54}$ $8\overline{)96}$ $5\overline{)85}$

5. $3\overline{)36}$ $6\overline{)24}$ $1\overline{)66}$ $6\overline{)78}$ $6\overline{)66}$

© RBP Books
www.summerbridgeactivities.com   Math Connection—Grade 5—RBP0172

Division
Divide.

Place the 1 in the hundreds column over the 5.

Place the 4 in the tens column over the 8.

$$4\overline{)584}$$

Here is another way to divide. **Think:** 4 times what number is closest to, but less than or equal to, 5?
$4 \times \mathbf{1} = 4$

$$\begin{array}{r} 1 \\ 4\overline{)584} \\ -4 \\ \hline 1 \end{array}$$

Bring down the 8 from the tens column.
Think: 4 times what number is closest to, but less than or equal to, 18?
$4 \times \mathbf{4} = 16$

$$\begin{array}{r} 14 \\ 4\overline{)584} \\ -4 \\ \hline 18 \\ -16 \\ \hline 2 \end{array}$$

Bring down the 4 from the ones column. **Think:** 4 times what is less than or equal to, 24?
$4 \times \mathbf{6} = 24$

$$\begin{array}{r} 146 \\ 4\overline{)584} \\ -4 \\ \hline 18 \\ -16 \\ \hline 24 \\ -24 \\ \hline 0 \end{array}$$

1. $5\overline{)600}$ $2\overline{)320}$ $6\overline{)168}$ $9\overline{)306}$ $3\overline{)846}$

2. $7\overline{)126}$ $5\overline{)190}$ $4\overline{)864}$ $6\overline{)306}$ $8\overline{)128}$

3. $4\overline{)448}$ $5\overline{)135}$ $1\overline{)154}$ $3\overline{)702}$ $2\overline{)204}$

4. $8\overline{)360}$ $5\overline{)525}$ $2\overline{)192}$ $3\overline{)792}$ $4\overline{)488}$

Math Connection—Grade 5—RBP0172   www.summerbridgeactivities.com   © RBP Books

Division
Divide.

Place 8 in the tens column to represent 80.

$$9\overline{)782}$$

Think: 9 times what number is close to, but less than or equal to, 782? (Round to guess.)

$9 \times \mathbf{80} = 720$

$$\begin{array}{r} 8 \\ 9\overline{)782} \\ -720 \\ \hline 62 \end{array}$$

Think: 9 times what number is close to, but less than or equal to, 62? (Round to guess.)

$9 \times \mathbf{6} = 54$

$$\begin{array}{r} 86 \\ 9\overline{)782} \\ -720 \\ \hline 62 \\ -54 \\ \hline 8 \end{array}$$

remainder

$$\begin{array}{r} 86\ \mathbf{R8} \\ 9\overline{)782} \end{array}$$

1. $5\overline{)58}$ $\quad 6\overline{)79}$ $\quad 8\overline{)15}$ $\quad 2\overline{)57}$ $\quad 3\overline{)78}$

2. $3\overline{)287}$ $\quad 9\overline{)498}$ $\quad 5\overline{)597}$ $\quad 1\overline{)286}$ $\quad 2\overline{)482}$

3. $4\overline{)782}$ $\quad 6\overline{)348}$ $\quad 9\overline{)963}$ $\quad 1\overline{)555}$ $\quad 4\overline{)489}$

4. $3\overline{)741}$ $\quad 7\overline{)219}$ $\quad 8\overline{)497}$ $\quad 7\overline{)741}$ $\quad 6\overline{)784}$

© RBP Books www.summerbridgeactivities.com **Math Connection—Grade 5—RBP0172**

Division
Divide.

Place 7 in the hundreds column over the 7.

Place 9 in the tens column over the 8.

```
          7                      79                    798 R1
6) 4,789   6) 4,789        6) 4,789        6) 4,789
           − 42                  − 4.2                 − 4.2
            5                     58                    58
                                − 54                   − 54
                                  4                     49
                                                       − 48
                                                         1
```

Think: Can you divide 4 by 6? No. Look at the next number in the dividend. Can you divide 47 by 6? Yes. 6 x **7** = 42

Bring down the 8. **Think:** 6 times what number is close to, but less than or equal to, 58? 6 x **9** = 54

Bring down the 9. **Think:** 6 times what number is close to, but less than or equal to, 49? 6 x **8** = 48

1. 6)9,773   5)2,668   8)6,433   7)6,301   8)8,057

2. 3)1,656   4)6,471   3)5,720   9)4,243   1)1,540

3. 9)5,006   6)9,378   2)1,040   1)4,416   8)5,745

4. 8)3,585   5)3,014   9)1,183   7)3,277   3)2,257

Math Connection—Grade 5—RBP0172   www.summerbridgeactivities.com   ©RBP Books

Division

Divide. Then check your answer.

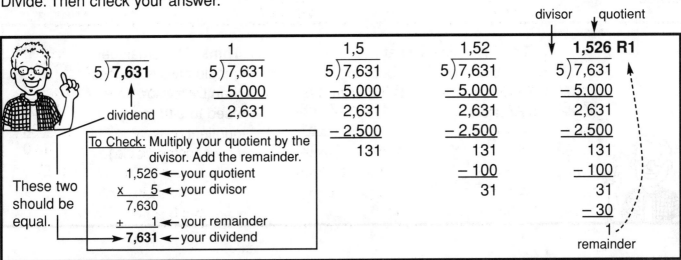

divisor   quotient

| | | | | **1,526 R1** |

To Check: Multiply your quotient by the divisor. Add the remainder.

```
1,526  ← your quotient
x     5  ← your divisor
7,630
+     1  ← your remainder
7,631  ← your dividend
```

These two should be equal.

remainder

---

1. 7)221   5)101   4)831

2. 9)762   2)332   8)890

3. 5)5,480   2)9,284   6)5,818

4. 6)1,587   9)1,377   3)1,116

Math Connection—Grade 5—RBP0172   www.summerbridgeactivities.com   ©RBP Books

Division

Divide.

$17\overline{)68}$

Think: 17 times what number is close to, but less than or equal to, 68? (Round to guess.)

20 x **?** = 70
20 x **3** = 60
17 x **3** = 51

Try 3:

$\begin{array}{r} 3 \\ 17\overline{)68} \\ -51 \\ \hline 17 \end{array}$

Think: My remainder should always be less than by divisor, so I need to add to my quotient. (Try 4 instead of 3.)

$\begin{array}{r} 4 \\ 17\overline{)68} \\ -68 \\ \hline 0 \end{array}$

1. $15\overline{)42}$ $23\overline{)47}$ $47\overline{)53}$ $25\overline{)60}$ $36\overline{)52}$

2. $11\overline{)22}$ $12\overline{)20}$ $17\overline{)27}$ $13\overline{)14}$ $20\overline{)20}$

3. $14\overline{)52}$ $12\overline{)48}$ $12\overline{)13}$ $17\overline{)25}$ $38\overline{)84}$

4. $34\overline{)74}$ $19\overline{)26}$ $46\overline{)97}$ $11\overline{)13}$ $26\overline{)88}$

© RBP Books   www.summerbridgeactivities.com   **Math Connection—Grade 5—RBP0172**

Division

Divide.

```
                                        1            12          121        121 R12
       72) 8,724      72) 8,724     72) 8,724    72) 8,724    72) 8,724
                       – 7,200       – 7,200      – 7,200      – 7,200
                         1,524         1,524        1,524        1,524
                                     – 1,440      – 1,440      – 1,440
                                          84           84           84
                                                     – 72         – 72
                                                       12           12
```

1. 92) 1,274   54) 2,809   98) 9,108   85) 3,910

2. 93) 7,728   87) 6,014   76) 6,975   32) 2,528

3. 74) 4,096   13) 3,412   30) 2,759   42) 6,803

4. 15) 1,080   85) 3,610   42) 2,976   31) 1,705

©RBP Books   www.summerbridgeactivities.com   Math Connection—Grade 5—RBP0172

Division

Divide.

1. $37\overline{)4{,}072}$ $81\overline{)4{,}455}$ $69\overline{)4{,}740}$ $52\overline{)3{,}486}$

2. $46\overline{)2{,}408}$ $21\overline{)1{,}240}$ $56\overline{)6{,}721}$ $17\overline{)7{,}147}$

3. $24\overline{)1{,}200}$ $82\overline{)5{,}832}$ $14\overline{)5{,}604}$ $35\overline{)1{,}610}$

4. $90\overline{)1{,}445}$ $67\overline{)5{,}655}$ $25\overline{)1{,}275}$ $61\overline{)2{,}135}$

5. $31\overline{)3{,}936}$ $29\overline{)3{,}009}$ $71\overline{)2{,}310}$ $60\overline{)5{,}520}$

6. $13\overline{)1{,}725}$ $47\overline{)1{,}036}$ $39\overline{)2{,}535}$ $85\overline{)2{,}150}$

Math Connection—Grade 5—RBP0172   www.summerbridgeactivities.com   ©RBP Books

Division

Divide.

	2	22	225	**2,255 R1**
26)58,631	26)58,63 − 52,000 6,631	26)58,631 − 52,000 6,631 − 5,200 1,431	26)58,631 − 52,000 6,631 − 5,200 1,431 − 1,300 131	26)58,631 − 52,000 6,631 − 5,200 1,431 − 1,300 131 − 130 1

1. 65)15,496   32)23,462   52)27,966   44)23,485

2. 29)20,202   72)42,921   54)42,_30   79)58,034

3. 91)91,119   53)51,430   32)27,215   17)38,774

© RBP Books   www.summerbridgeactivities.com   Math Connection—Grade _ -RBP0172

Division

Divide. Then check your answer.

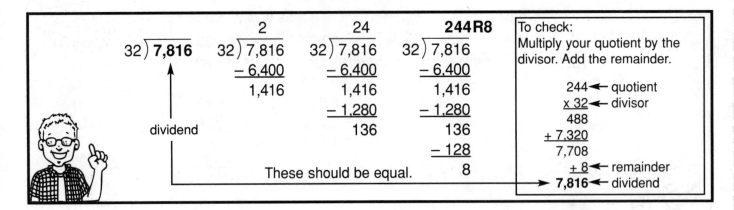

1.   43)9,551   58)8,150   26)3,140

2.   34)9,607   44)1,125   87)46,752

3.   45)24,497   60)52,960   74)15,665

It's better than dividing!

Math Connection—Grade 5—RBP0172   www.summerbridgeactivities.com   ©RBP Books

Problem Solving

1. Tyree is studying the typical ages of different animals. His dad told him that his dog, Sparky, is 91 in dog years. If 1 human year is equal to 7 dog years, how many human years has Sparky been alive?

2. Camille states that her dog is only 56 dog years old. How many years old is Camille's dog?

3. Katrina found out that 1 human year is about 5 cat years. Her veterinarian told her that her cat was probably about 38 cat years old.
   a. How old is Katrina's cat in human years?

   b. What is the remainder?

4. George found out that 1 human year is about 25 rat years. Jason claims that his rat must be 208 rat years!
   a. How many human years old would Jason's rat be in order for his claim to be correct?

   b. What would the remainder be?

5. Latisha asked her teacher, Mrs. Sandall, how old she was. Mrs. Sandall responded that she is 10,764 days old. Assuming that there are 365 days in a year,
   a. How many years old is Mrs. Sandall?

   b. How many days are there until her next birthday?

©RBP Books
www.summerbridgeactivities.com
Math Connection—Grade 5—RBP0172

Problem Solving

Use the story below to solve the problems.

Martin mows lawns in the summer for some of his neighbors. He decided save all his money and not spend any of his earnings.

1. Last summer, Martin charged his neighbors $12 each time he mowed their lawn. He earned a total of $732 over the summer. How many lawns did he mow?

2. Next year, Martin has decided to begin fertilizing lawns. A 20-pound bag of fertilizer will be enough fertilizer for 5,000 square feet. How many square feet can each pound of fertilizer cover?

3. If Martin plans on mowing 70 lawns next summer, how much must he charge if he wants to earn $910?

4. Martin mowed 5 lawns on one Saturday at $12 per lawn. At the end of the day, he counted up his money. He had $62. He remembered that Mrs. Wilson had given him a tip. How much of a tip did she give him?

5. Martin's sister Mindy wants to earn some extra money next summer, too. She plans on baby-sitting. She wants to earn $720 over the course of the summer.
   a. If Mindy charges $5 an hour, how many hours will she have to baby-sit?

   b. If there are 12 weeks during her summer break, how many hours a week on average will she have to work?

Post-Test: Division

1. $3\overline{)93}$ $4\overline{)78}$ $6\overline{)375}$ $5\overline{)687}$

2. $3\overline{)4{,}418}$ $8\overline{)7{,}243}$ $26\overline{)87}$ $12\overline{)74}$

3. $27\overline{)61}$ $26\overline{)78}$ $41\overline{)123}$ $62\overline{)753}$

4. $24\overline{)430}$ $45\overline{)378}$ $82\overline{)7{,}457}$ $37\overline{)5{,}775}$

5. $45\overline{)2{,}875}$ $88\overline{)7{,}638}$ $89\overline{)19{,}876}$ $32\overline{)67{,}814}$

© RBP Books   www.summerbridgeactivities.com   Math Connection—Grade 5—RBP0172

Standard Length

| 1 foot (ft.) is equal to 12 inches (in.). |
| 1 yard (yd.) is equal to 3 feet. |
| 1 mile (mi.) is equal to 5,280 feet. |

---

3 ft. = _____ in.

if   1 ft = 12 in.
then   3 ft = (3 x 12) in. = 36 in.

3 ft. = __**36**__ in.

---

48 in. = _____ ft.

if   12 in. = 1 ft.
then   48 in. = (48 ÷ 12) ft. = 4 ft.

48 in. = __**4**__ ft.

---

6 yd. 4 ft. = _____ ft.

if   1 yd. = 3 ft.
then   6 yd. = (6 x 3) ft. = 18 ft.
so   6 yd. 4 ft. = 18 + 4 ft.

6 yd. 4 ft. = __**22**__ ft.

Circle the best answer.

1. The length of a desk   3 in.   3 ft.   3 yd.   3 mi.

2. The height of an adult   68 in.   68 ft.   68 yd.   68 mi.

3. The length of a pencil   8 in.   8 ft.   8 yd.   8 mi.

4. The distance around 10 blocks   2 in.   2 ft.   2 yd.   2 mi.

5. The height of a full grown oak tree   5 in.   5 ft.   5 yd.   5 mi.

Complete.

6.   60 in. = _____ ft.   5 ft. = _____ in.

7.   2 yd. = _____ ft.   4 yd. 2 ft. = _____ ft.

8.   2 mi. = _____ ft.   72 in. = _____ ft.

9.   6 yd. 2 ft. = _____ ft.   2 ft. 10 in. = _____ in.

10.   7 ft. 3 in. = _____ in.   36 in. = _____ ft.

11.   8 yd. 7 ft. = _____ ft.   3 mi. 310 ft. = _____ ft.

12.   84 in. = _____ ft.   13 ft. 2 in. = _____ in.

13.   5 mi. 143 ft. = _____ ft.   21 yd. 6 ft. = _____ ft.

Math Connection—Grade 5—RBP0172   www.summerbridgeactivities.com   ©RBP Books

Standard Capacity and Weight

| 1 pint (pt.) is equal to 2 cups. |
| 1 quart (qt.) is equal to 2 pints. |
| 1 gallon (gal.) is equal to 4 quarts. |
| 1 pound (lb.) is equal to 16 ounces. |

3 pt. = _____ cups	8 qt. = _____ gal.	2 gal. 3 qt. = _____ qt.
if 1 pt. = 2 cups then 3 pt. = (3 x 2) cups = 6 cups	if 4 qt. = 1 gal. then 8 qt. = (8 ÷ 4) gal. = 2 gal.	if 1 gal. = 4 quarts then 2 gal. = (2 x 4) qt. = 8 qt. so 2 gal. 3 qt. = 8 + 3 qt.
3 pt. = __6__ cups	8 qt. = __2__ gal.	2 gal. 3 qt. = __11__ qt.

Circle the best answer.

1. The capacity of a glass   2 cups   2 pt.   2 qt.   2 gal.

2. The capacity of a tub   60 cups   60 pt.   60 qt.   60 gal.

3. The capacity of a sink   2 cups   2 pt.   2 qt.   2 gal.

4. The capacity of a pitcher   2 cups   2 pt.   2 qt.   2 gal.

Complete.

5.   5 pt. = _____ cups   4 pt. = _____ qt.

6.   2 qt. = _____ pt.   32 oz. = _____ lb.

7.   3 gal. = _____ qt.   8 cups = _____ pt.

8.   5 lb. 8 oz. = _____ oz.   4 pt. 1 cup = _____ cups

9.   4 qt. 1 pt. = _____ pt.   16 qt. = _____ gal.

10.   5 pt. 1 cup = _____ cups   12 pt. = _____ cups

11.   22 pt. = _____ qt.   8 lb. 7 oz. = _____ oz.

12.   14 qt. 1 pt. = _____ pt.   20 cups = _____ pt.

©RBP Books   www.summerbridgeactivities.com   Math Connection—Grade 5—RBP0172

Standard Measurement

Use the information on the previous two pages to solve the following.

1. Allison bought 1 gallon of milk. She had a recipe that called for 1 quart of milk. How much milk does she have left?

2. Jake has 1 pound of cheese. He puts 6 ounces onto a pizza he is making. How many ounces of cheese does he have left?

3. Keaton bought a pint of ice cream. How many cups of ice cream does he have?

4. Gabriel ran for 1 mile. Then he started jogging. He jogged for 250 feet. How many total feet did he run and jog?

5. A football field is 100 yards long. How many feet is that?

6. Lorenzo purchased 2 gallons of chocolate milk. Dylan purchased 6 quarts of chocolate milk.
   a. How many quarts of chocolate milk did Lorenzo purchase?

   b. Who has more chocolate milk?

   c. By how much?

7. Derek has 2 feet of Tasty Cherry Rope. He plans on splitting it evenly between himself and 5 of his friends.
   a. How many inches of Tasty Cherry Rope does Derek have?

   b. How many inches should each person get?

8. Joyce has 3 pounds of jelly beans. If she gives 4 ounces to each person, how many people can she give her jelly beans to?

Pre-Test: Fractions

Write the fraction for the part that is shaded.

1.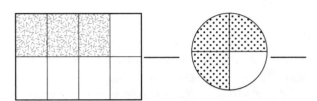

Change each improper fraction to a mixed number.

2. $\dfrac{8}{3}$ $\dfrac{7}{5}$ $\dfrac{9}{2}$

_____   _____   _____

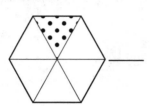

Change each mixed number to an improper fraction.

3. $2\dfrac{3}{4}$ $4\dfrac{3}{7}$ $5\dfrac{1}{2}$

_____   _____   _____

Simplify the following fractions.

4. $\dfrac{4}{6}$ $\dfrac{5}{15}$ $\dfrac{4}{18}$

_____   _____   _____

Simplify each mixed number. Leave as a mixed number.

5. $1\dfrac{3}{12}$ $4\dfrac{4}{8}$ $8\dfrac{6}{9}$

_____   _____   _____

Rewrite each fraction.

6. $\dfrac{3}{4}\ \overline{16}$ $\dfrac{2}{3}\ \overline{21}$ $\dfrac{1}{6}\ \overline{18}$

_____   _____   _____

© RBP Books   www.summerbridgeactivities.com   Math Connection—Grade 5—RBP0172

Fractions

A fraction is a part of a whole.

$\frac{3}{4}$ of the circle is shaded. $\frac{1}{4}$ of the circle is not shaded.

$\frac{3}{4}$ ← part shaded   numerator   part not shaded ⟶ $\frac{1}{4}$
   ← total parts   denominator   total parts ⟶

$\frac{4}{5}$ of the rectangle is shaded.

$\frac{1}{5}$ of the rectangle is not shaded.

On the first line, write the fraction for the part that is shaded.

On the second line write the fraction for the part that is not shaded.

1.

$\frac{3}{8}$ $\frac{5}{8}$ ___ ___   ___ ___   ___ ___

2.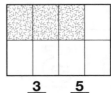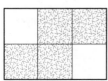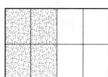

___ ___   ___ ___   ___ ___   ___ ___

3.

___   ___   ___   ___

4.

___ ___   ___ ___   ___ ___   ___ ___

Math Connection—Grade 5—RBP0172   www.summerbridgeactivities.com   ©RBP Books

Fractions

Color in the following fractions.

 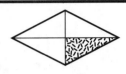 $\frac{1}{4}$ of the diamond is shaded. $\frac{4}{8}$ or $\frac{1}{2}$ of the circle is shaded.

1. $\frac{1}{2}$ $\frac{3}{4}$ $\frac{1}{4}$

2. $\frac{3}{4}$  $\frac{1}{4}$  $\frac{4}{4}$

3. $\frac{7}{8}$ 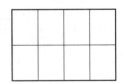 $\frac{2}{8}$  $\frac{3}{8}$

4. $\frac{2}{3}$ $\frac{1}{3}$ $\frac{3}{3}$

5. $\frac{5}{8}$ $\frac{2}{8}$ $\frac{1}{4}$

6. $\frac{4}{6}$ $\frac{5}{6}$ $\frac{2}{3}$

©RBP Books   www.summerbridgeactivities.com   Math Connection—Grade 5—RBP0172

Fractions

 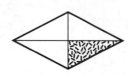

$\frac{1}{4}$ of the rectangle is shaded.

$\frac{1}{4}$ is read as **one-fourth**.

$\frac{2}{3}$ of the circle is <u>not</u> shaded.

$\frac{2}{3}$ is read as **two-thirds**.

Write the following words as fractions.

1. three-fifths $\qquad \dfrac{3}{5} \qquad$ three-fourths _____

2. four-ninths _____   one-fourth _____

3. one-third _____   six-twelfths _____

4. two-eighths _____   four-tenths _____

5. four-fifths _____   five-elevenths _____

6. one-half _____   seven-eighths _____

Write the words for each of the given fractions.

7. $\frac{1}{3}$ $\qquad$ **one-third** $\qquad$ $\frac{2}{3}$ _____

8. $\frac{1}{2}$ _____ $\frac{1}{8}$ _____

9. $\frac{3}{8}$ _____ $\frac{4}{11}$ _____

10. $\frac{2}{5}$ _____ $\frac{5}{3}$ _____

11. $\frac{5}{7}$ _____ $\frac{5}{9}$ _____

12. $\frac{4}{3}$ _____ $\frac{9}{2}$ _____

www.summerbridgeactivities.com   © RBP Books

Changing Improper Fractions to Mixed Numbers

Change the improper fractions to mixed numbers.

$\frac{14}{3}$ can be rewritten as $14 \div 3$ or $3\overline{)14}$

$\frac{14}{3}$ is an improper fraction.

$\begin{array}{r} 4 \ \text{R2} \\ 3\overline{)14} \\ -12 \\ \hline 2 \end{array}$ $\frac{14}{3} = 4\frac{2}{3}$ 2 becomes the numerator; the denominator stays 3.

$4\frac{2}{3}$ is a mixed number.

1. $\frac{15}{2}$ _____ $\frac{7}{4}$ _____ $\frac{20}{7}$ _____

2. $\frac{43}{5}$ _____ $\frac{23}{8}$ _____ $\frac{21}{5}$ _____

3. $\frac{31}{12}$ _____ $\frac{5}{2}$ _____ $\frac{13}{8}$ _____

4. $\frac{11}{4}$ _____ $\frac{49}{9}$ _____ $\frac{41}{6}$ _____

5. $\frac{23}{3}$ _____ $\frac{45}{4}$ _____ $\frac{60}{5}$ _____

6. $\frac{23}{7}$ _____ $\frac{72}{6}$ _____ $\frac{16}{2}$ _____

©RBP Books   www.summerbridgeactivities.com   Math Connection—Grade 5—RBP0172

Changing Improper Fractions to Mixed Numbers

Change the improper fractions to mixed or whole numbers.

1. $\dfrac{5}{4}$ $\dfrac{7}{2}$ $\dfrac{6}{5}$

2. $\dfrac{8}{3}$ $\dfrac{9}{2}$ $\dfrac{12}{5}$

3. $\dfrac{9}{5}$ $\dfrac{62}{7}$ $\dfrac{14}{3}$

4. $\dfrac{12}{5}$ $\dfrac{80}{10}$ $\dfrac{89}{12}$

5. $\dfrac{10}{3}$ $\dfrac{71}{9}$ $\dfrac{61}{6}$

6. $\dfrac{13}{2}$ $\dfrac{54}{5}$ $\dfrac{9}{7}$

7. $\dfrac{49}{12}$ $\dfrac{100}{10}$ $\dfrac{82}{11}$

8. $\dfrac{47}{12}$ $\dfrac{58}{9}$ $\dfrac{97}{10}$

My goodness, these fractions are improper!

Math Connection—Grade 5—RBP0172   www.summerbridgeactivities.com   ©RBP Books

Name _____   Date _____

Changing Mixed Numbers to Improper Fractions

$3\frac{1}{3} = \frac{(3 \times 3) + 1}{3}$

$= \frac{9 + 1}{3}$

$= \frac{10}{3}$

To change mixed numbers to improper fractions:

1. Multiply the denominator by the whole number.
2. Add the numerator.
3. Keep the denominator.

$4\frac{5}{8} = \frac{(8 \times 4) + 5}{8}$

$= \frac{32 + 5}{8}$

$= \frac{37}{8}$

Change the mixed numbers to improper fractions.

1. $2\frac{1}{3}$ $6\frac{3}{4}$ $1\frac{1}{12}$

2. $3\frac{1}{8}$ $7\frac{3}{5}$ $1\frac{9}{10}$

3. $3\frac{2}{5}$ $9\frac{4}{11}$ $3\frac{6}{7}$

4. $5\frac{4}{5}$ $4\frac{5}{12}$ $6\frac{7}{11}$

© RBP Books www.summerbridgeactivities.com   Math Connection—Grade 5—RBP0172

Changing Mixed Numbers to Improper Fractions

Change the following mixed numbers to improper fractions.

1. $3\frac{4}{5}$ $2\frac{3}{8}$ $1\frac{5}{12}$

2. $2\frac{5}{8}$ $5\frac{3}{4}$ $8\frac{1}{9}$

3. $4\frac{2}{3}$ $6\frac{1}{2}$ $12\frac{5}{9}$

4. $7\frac{1}{8}$ $1\frac{5}{7}$ $4\frac{8}{11}$

5. $6\frac{3}{7}$ $3\frac{2}{5}$ $7\frac{11}{12}$

6. $6\frac{7}{8}$ $2\frac{7}{12}$ $5\frac{3}{10}$

Hey! There's only a fraction of this pie left!

74

Simplifying Fractions

$$\frac{4}{8} = \frac{4 \div 4}{8 \div 4}$$

$$= \frac{1}{2}$$

A fraction is simplified when 1 is the only number that divides into both the numerator and the denominator.

To simplify, you must divide the numerator and denominator by the same number.

$$\frac{12}{18} = \frac{12 \div 2}{18 \div 2}$$

$$= \frac{6}{9}$$

$\frac{6}{9}$ is not simplified.

$$\frac{6}{9} = \frac{6 \div 3}{9 \div 3}$$

$$= \frac{2}{3}$$

Simplify.

1. $\dfrac{4}{8}$ $\dfrac{6}{15}$ $\dfrac{8}{24}$

2. $\dfrac{4}{6}$ $\dfrac{5}{15}$ $\dfrac{6}{10}$

3. $\dfrac{6}{8}$ $\dfrac{2}{24}$ $\dfrac{8}{12}$

4. $\dfrac{3}{9}$ $\dfrac{6}{24}$ $\dfrac{10}{12}$

5. $\dfrac{6}{12}$ $\dfrac{5}{20}$ $\dfrac{14}{14}$

© RBP Books   www.summerbridgeactivities.com   Math Connection—Grade 5—RBP0172

Simplifying Fractions

It's better than dividing!

Simplify.

1. $\dfrac{15}{30}$ $\dfrac{55}{66}$ $\dfrac{16}{48}$

2. $\dfrac{10}{24}$ $\dfrac{6}{72}$ $\dfrac{24}{36}$

3. $\dfrac{10}{35}$ $\dfrac{2}{18}$ $\dfrac{8}{24}$

4. $\dfrac{4}{8}$ $\dfrac{54}{54}$ $\dfrac{9}{27}$

5. $\dfrac{7}{21}$ $\dfrac{15}{25}$ $\dfrac{25}{50}$

6. $\dfrac{6}{18}$ $\dfrac{9}{12}$ $\dfrac{2}{16}$

7. $\dfrac{18}{27}$ $\dfrac{14}{40}$ $\dfrac{9}{18}$

8. $\dfrac{6}{15}$ $\dfrac{12}{36}$ $\dfrac{6}{9}$

    www.summerbridgeactivities.com   © RBP Books

Simplifying Mixed Numbers

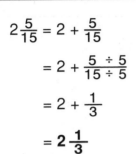

$$2\frac{5}{15} = 2 + \frac{5}{15}$$
$$= 2 + \frac{5 \div 5}{15 \div 5}$$
$$= 2 + \frac{1}{3}$$
$$= 2\frac{1}{3}$$

When simplifying mixed numbers, simplify the fraction.

$$3\frac{9}{6} = 3 + \frac{9}{6}$$
$$= 3 + \frac{9 \div 3}{6 \div 3}$$
$$= 3 + \frac{3}{2}$$

Change to a mixed number.

$$= 3 + 1\frac{1}{2}$$
$$= 3 + 1 + \frac{1}{2} = 4\frac{1}{2}$$

Simplify.

1. $2\frac{2}{4}$ $3\frac{5}{15}$ $2\frac{12}{16}$

2. $1\frac{6}{9}$ $2\frac{9}{2}$ $6\frac{3}{3}$

3. $2\frac{5}{20}$ $4\frac{7}{21}$ $5\frac{9}{6}$

4. $4\frac{9}{3}$ $5\frac{3}{12}$ $2\frac{3}{2}$

© RBP Books   www.summerbridgeactivities.com   Math Connection—Grade 5—RBP0172

Simplest Form

Simplify.

1. $\dfrac{6}{18}$ $\dfrac{12}{18}$ $\dfrac{20}{24}$

2. $\dfrac{18}{24}$ $\dfrac{9}{54}$ $\dfrac{6}{12}$

Write each of the following as a mixed number in simplest form.

3. $\dfrac{9}{8}$ $\dfrac{11}{5}$ $\dfrac{16}{6}$

4. $\dfrac{16}{3}$ $\dfrac{24}{16}$ $\dfrac{18}{4}$

5. $1\dfrac{5}{15}$ $2\dfrac{4}{6}$ $4\dfrac{3}{12}$

6. $5\dfrac{8}{6}$ $4\dfrac{18}{24}$ $3\dfrac{9}{2}$

Math Connection—Grade 5—RBP0172   www.summerbridgeactivities.com   © RBP Books

Renaming Fractions

To rename a fraction, multiply the numerator and denominator by the same number.

$$\frac{1}{3} = \frac{1 \times 2}{3 \times 2} = \frac{2}{6}$$

$\frac{1}{3}$ of the circle is shaded.

$\frac{2}{6}$ of the circle is shaded.

$$\frac{4}{5} \longrightarrow \frac{}{10}$$

Think: To get from 5 to 10, multiply by 2.

So, $\frac{4}{5} = \frac{4 \times 2}{5 \times 2} = \frac{8}{10}$

$$\frac{2}{3} \longrightarrow \frac{}{12}$$

Think: To get from 3 to 12, multiply by 4.

So, $\frac{2}{3} = \frac{2 \times 4}{3 \times 4} = \frac{8}{12}$

Rename the following fractions using the denominator given.

1. $\frac{3}{4} = \frac{}{12}$ $\frac{4}{5} = \frac{}{15}$ $\frac{2}{3} = \frac{}{6}$

2. $\frac{1}{4} = \frac{}{16}$ $\frac{5}{6} = \frac{}{18}$ $\frac{3}{5} = \frac{}{20}$

I ♡ fractions!

3. $\frac{5}{8} = \frac{}{24}$ $\frac{2}{7} = \frac{}{14}$ $\frac{5}{6} = \frac{}{12}$

© RBP Books   www.summerbridgeactivities.com   Math Connection—Grade 5—RBP0172

Renaming Fractions

$\frac{2}{5} = \overline{15}$

So, $\frac{2}{5} = \frac{2 \times 3}{5 \times 3} = \frac{6}{15}$

$4 = \frac{}{2}$ Think of 4 as $\frac{4}{1}$.

$\frac{4}{1} = \frac{}{2}$

So, $\frac{4}{1} = \frac{4 \times 2}{1 \times 2} = \frac{8}{2}$

Rewrite each fraction using the denominator given.

1. $\quad \frac{1}{2} = \frac{}{8}$ $\qquad\qquad \frac{2}{3} = \frac{}{30}$ $\qquad\qquad \frac{3}{4} = \frac{}{20}$

2. $\quad \frac{3}{5} = \frac{}{15}$ $\qquad\qquad \frac{1}{5} = \frac{}{50}$ $\qquad\qquad \frac{11}{12} = \frac{}{48}$

3. $\quad \frac{1}{4} = \frac{}{12}$ $\qquad\qquad \frac{4}{9} = \frac{}{81}$ $\qquad\qquad \frac{5}{9} = \frac{}{18}$

4. $\quad \frac{1}{3} = \frac{}{15}$ $\qquad\qquad \frac{2}{7} = \frac{}{21}$ $\qquad\qquad \frac{3}{4} = \frac{}{16}$

Math Connection—Grade 5—RBP0172   www.summerbridgeactivities.com   © RBP Books

Using the LCD to Write Equivalent Fractions

The least common denominator (LCD) for two fractions is the smallest common multiple of the denominators.

To find the LCD:
1. List the multiples of each denominator.
2. The LCD is the smallest common multiple.

Example: Find the LCD of $\frac{2}{3}$ and $\frac{3}{4}$. Rewrite each fraction using the LCD.

1.   List the multiples of each denominator.

   $3 = 3, 6, 9, \textcircled{12}\ 15, 18, 21, 24,\dots$

   $4 = 4, 8, \textcircled{12}\ 16, 20, 24,\dots$

2.   The LCD = 12.

$\frac{2}{3} = \frac{}{12}$ ◄——The LCD of 3 and 4 $\frac{3}{4} = \frac{}{12}$ ◄—— The LCD of 3 and 4

$\frac{2}{3} = \frac{2\times4}{3\times4} = \frac{8}{12}$ $\frac{3}{4} = \frac{3\times3}{4\times3} = \frac{9}{12}$

$\frac{2}{3} = \frac{8}{12}$ $\frac{3}{4} = \frac{9}{12}$

Find the LCD of each pair of fractions.

Then rewrite each fraction using the new common denominator.

1. $\frac{2}{3}, \frac{4}{5}$ $\frac{1}{2}, \frac{1}{3}$ $\frac{2}{5}, \frac{1}{2}$

2. $\frac{3}{4}, \frac{1}{5}$ $\frac{1}{7}, \frac{2}{3}$ $\frac{6}{7}, \frac{1}{3}$

3. $\frac{1}{2}, \frac{3}{5}$ $\frac{4}{7}, \frac{1}{2}$ $\frac{2}{3}, \frac{5}{8}$

©RBP Books   www.summerbridgeactivities.com   Math Connection—Grade 5—RBP0172

Using the LCD to Write Equivalent Fractions

Find the LCD of $\frac{1}{4}$ and $\frac{3}{8}$. Rewrite each fraction using the LCD.

1. List the multiples of each denominator.

$4 = 4, \textcircled{8}, 12, 16, 20, 24, \ldots$

$8 = \textcircled{8}, 16, 24, \ldots$

To find the LCD:
1. List the multiples of each denominator.
2. The LCD is the smallest common multiple.

2. The LCD = 8.

$\frac{1}{4} = \frac{}{8}$ ⟵ The LCD of 4 and 8

$\frac{1}{4} = \frac{1 \times 2}{4 \times 2} = \frac{2}{8}$

$\frac{1}{4} = \frac{2}{8}$

$\frac{3}{8} = \frac{}{8}$ ⟵ The LCD of 4 and 8

$\frac{3}{8} = \frac{3 \times 1}{8 \times 1} = \frac{3}{8}$

$\frac{3}{8} = \frac{3}{8}$

Find the LCD of each pair of fractions.

Then rewrite each fraction using the new common denominator.

1. $\frac{2}{3}, \frac{5}{6}$ $\frac{1}{2}, \frac{1}{4}$ $\frac{2}{5}, \frac{1}{10}$

2. $\frac{3}{4}, \frac{1}{12}$ $\frac{1}{7}, \frac{2}{14}$ $\frac{6}{9}, \frac{1}{3}$

3. $\frac{1}{10}, \frac{3}{5}$ $\frac{3}{8}, \frac{1}{2}$ $\frac{3}{4}, \frac{5}{8}$

Using the LCD to Write Equivalent Fractions

Find the LCD of $\frac{1}{4}$ and $\frac{5}{6}$. Rewrite each fraction using the LCD.

1. List the multiples of each denominator.

   4 = 4, 8, ⑫, 16, 20, 24,…

   6 = 6, ⑫ 18, 24,…

2. The LCD = 12.

$\frac{1}{4} = \frac{}{12}$ ⟵——— The LCD of 4 and 6 $\frac{5}{6} = \frac{}{12}$ ⟵——— The LCD of 4 and 6

$\frac{1}{4} = \frac{1 \times 3}{4 \times 3} = \frac{3}{12}$ $\frac{5}{6} = \frac{5 \times 2}{6 \times 2} = \frac{10}{12}$

$\frac{1}{4} = \frac{3}{12}$ $\frac{5}{6} = \frac{10}{12}$

Find the LCD of each pair of fractions.

Then rewrite each fraction using the new common denominator.

1. $\frac{1}{6}, \frac{5}{8}$ $\frac{1}{4}, \frac{1}{6}$ $\frac{2}{6}, \frac{1}{18}$

2. $\frac{3}{4}, \frac{1}{10}$ $\frac{1}{8}, \frac{2}{12}$ $\frac{2}{3}, \frac{1}{12}$

3. $\frac{7}{10}, \frac{3}{6}$ $\frac{3}{8}, \frac{1}{10}$ $\frac{3}{4}, \frac{5}{6}$

© RBP Books   www.summerbridgeactivities.com   Math Connection—Grade 5—RBP0172

Problem Solving

Math-Balls

$2\frac{1}{2}$ cups peanut butter

$1\frac{2}{8}$ cups honey

two and one-half teaspoons vanilla

$5\frac{5}{2}$ cups coconut

$\frac{5}{2}$ cups raisins

You want to make Math-Balls, but you only have 3 measuring cups—a 1 cup, $\frac{1}{4}$ cup, and $\frac{1}{3}$ cup.

1. You measure 2 cups of peanut butter into the mixing bowl. How many $\frac{1}{4}$ cups will you need to complete the recipe?

2. Will you use your $\frac{1}{4}$ cup or $\frac{1}{3}$ cup to measure the honey?

3. Write the mixed number for the amount of vanilla you will need to add.

4. How many cups of coconut will you need to add? (Do not include an improper fraction.)

5. How many cups of raisins will you need? (Do not include an improper fraction.)

6. What ingredient do you add the most of?

Math Connection—Grade 5—RBP0172   www.summerbridgeactivities.com   ©RBP Books

Post-Test: Fractions

Change each improper fraction to a mixed number.

1. $\dfrac{7}{3}$ $\dfrac{11}{5}$ $\dfrac{5}{2}$ $\dfrac{9}{8}$

Change each mixed number to an improper fraction.

2. $1\dfrac{3}{5}$ $4\dfrac{2}{3}$ $5\dfrac{1}{6}$ $3\dfrac{5}{8}$

Simplify the following fractions.

3. $\dfrac{15}{20}$ $\dfrac{4}{12}$ $\dfrac{2}{16}$ $\dfrac{6}{20}$

Simplify each mixed number. Leave as a mixed number.

4. $2\dfrac{9}{12}$ $3\dfrac{6}{8}$ $6\dfrac{6}{18}$ $1\dfrac{8}{20}$

Rewrite each fraction.

5. $\dfrac{1}{4} = \dfrac{}{12}$ $\dfrac{4}{6} = \dfrac{}{24}$ $\dfrac{4}{5} = \dfrac{}{25}$ $\dfrac{2}{9} = \dfrac{}{27}$

© RBP Books   www.summerbridgeactivities.com   Math Connection—Grade 5—RBP0172

Metric Length

1 meter (m) is about the length of a baseball bat.	1 millimeter (mm) is about the width of a head on a pin.
← 1 meter → 	→ ← 1 millimeter 
1 centimeter (cm) is about the width of your finger.	1 kilometer (km) is just over a half a mile.
← 1 centimeter	← 1 kilometer →

Circle the best measurement.

1. height of a house   11 m   11 cm   width of a staple   1 cm   1 mm

2. height of a 5-year-old   1 km   1 m   length of a pencil   18 m   18 cm

3. height of this page   28 mm   28 cm   height of a door   2 m   2 km

4. piece of dust   1 cm   1 mm   distance to the moon   350,000 km 350,000 mm

5. Would you measure the height of a tree in   mm   cm   m   km?

6. Would you measure the distance from New York to California in   mm   cm   m   km?

7. Would you measure the length of a spoon in   mm   cm   m   km?

8. Would you measure the length of an ant in   mm   cm   m   km?

9. Would you measure the height of a tall building in   mm   cm   m   km?

10. Would you measure the length of a paper clip in   mm   cm   m   km?

Math Connection—Grade 5—RBP0172   www.summerbridgeactivities.com   © RBP Books

Metric Length

| 1 kilometer (km) = 1,000 meters (m) |
| 1 meter (m) = 100 centimeters (cm) |
| 1 centimeter (cm) = 10 millimeters (mm) |

To go from a larger to a smaller unit, multiply.

To go from a smaller to a larger unit, divide.

$5 \text{ m} =$ _____ cm
Think: 1 m = 100 cm
So, 5 m = 5 x 100 cm
$5 \text{ m} = \textbf{500 cm}$

$520 \text{ mm} =$ _____ cm
Think: 10 mm = 1 cm
So, 520 mm = (520 ÷ 10) cm
$520 \text{ mm} = \textbf{52 cm}$

$72,000 \text{ m} =$ _____ km
Think: 1,000 m = 1 km
So, 72,000 m = (72,000 ÷ 1,000) km
$72,000 \text{ m} = \textbf{72 km}$

Complete.

1. 42 m = _____ cm   620 mm = _____ cm

2. 4 km = _____ m   8,000 m = _____ km

3. 85 cm = _____ mm   5,400 mm = _____ cm

4. If Caylee is 102 centimeters, is she > or < 1 meter?

5. Your dresser is 196 centimeters wide. Will it fit along a wall that is 2 meters long?

6. Dylan has a roll of wrapping paper that is 5 meters long. How many centimeters of wrapping paper does he have?

7. The Kilgore family traveled 35,000 meters to get to the nearest amusement park. How many kilometers did they have to travel?

© RBP Books   www.summerbridgeactivities.com   Math Connection—Grade 5—RBP0172

Metric Capacity

1 kl = 1,000 l
1 l = 1,000 ml

Liter (l) is the basic metric unit for capacity.
1 liter (l) is about $4\frac{1}{4}$ cups.
1,000 millimeters is equal to 1 liter.

1 kiloliter (kl) is equal to 1,000 liters. It would take 500 2-liter pop bottles to equal one kiloliter.

1 milliliter (ml) is very small. It is about $\frac{1}{5}$ of a teaspoon.

7 kl = _____ l
Think: 1 kl = 1,000 l
So, 7 kl = (7 x 1,000) l
7 kl = **7,000 l**

8,000 ml = _____ l
Think: 1,000 ml = 1 L
So, 8,000 ml = (8,000 ÷ 1,000) l
8,000 ml = **8 l**

Circle the best measurement.

1. capacity of a gallon of milk   3.8 ml   3.8 l   one teaspoon vanilla   5 ml   5 l

2. two bathtubs of water   100 l   1 kl   dropper of medicine   1 ml   1 l

Complete.

3. 2 kl = _____ l   2000 ml = _____ l

4. 5 l = _____ ml   45,000 l = _____ kl

5. 24 kl = _____ l   38 l = _____ ml

6. Emily is making juice from frozen concentrate. The package says it makes 2 liters.
   a. How many milliliters is that?

   b. If one serving size is 250 ml, how many servings does the package make?

Metric Mass

The word *mass* is similar to the word *weight*.

1 gram (g) is about the mass of a dollar bill.

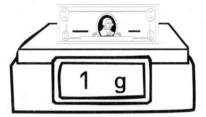

1 g

1 kilogram (kg) is used to measure the mass of larger objects. A newborn baby would usually weigh 3 to 4 kilograms.

4 kg

1,000 grams (g) = 1 kilogram (kg)

Circle the best measurement.

1. a sack of potatoes   5 kg   5 g   a quarter   6 g   6 kg

2. a cat $3\frac{1}{2}$ g $3\frac{1}{2}$ kg   a fifth grader   34 g   34 kg

Complete.

3. 7 kg = _____ g   6,000 g = _____kg

4. 12 kg = _____ g   73,000 g = _____ kg

5. An extra-large pizza weighs 2 kilograms. How many grams does it weigh?

6. If the pizza in the above problem is divided equally into 8 slices, how many grams does each slice weigh?

7. If a child's stomach can only hold 750 grams of pizza, how many slices of pizza can it hold?

©RBP Books   www.summerbridgeactivities.com   **Math Connection—Grade 5—RBP0172**

Reading a Metric Ruler

You will need a metric ruler to measure the following.

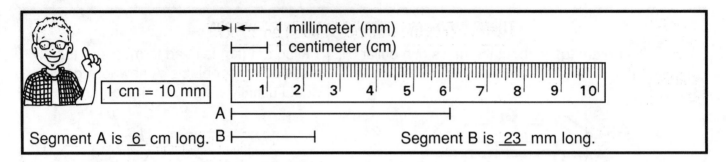

Measure to the nearest centimeter (cm).

1.

2.

3.

4.

Measure to the nearest millimeter (mm).

5.

6.

7.

Draw a line for the following measurements.

8. 27 mm

9. 6 cm

10. 5 cm and 8 mm

Perimeter

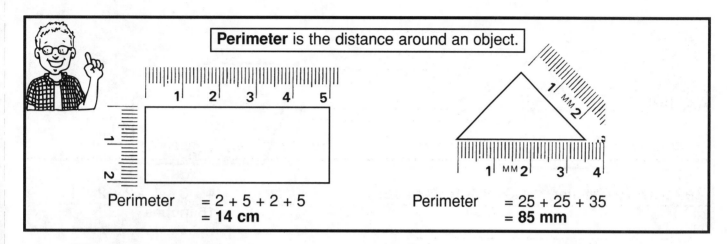

Perimeter is the distance around an object.

Perimeter   = 2 + 5 + 2 + 5
          = **14 cm**

Perimeter   = 25 + 25 + 35
          = **85 mm**

Measure the length of each side to find the perimeter in centimeters.

1.

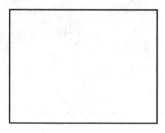

_____cm

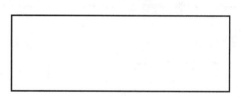

_____cm

2.

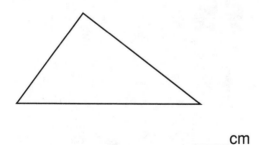

_____cm

_____cm

Measure the length of each side to find the perimeter in millimeters.

3.

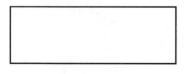

_____mm

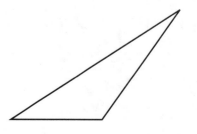

_____mm

© RBP Books   www.summerbridgeactivities.com   Math Connection—Grade 5—RBP0172

Perimeter

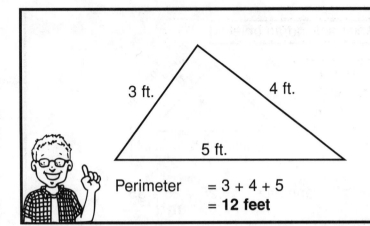

Perimeter   = 3 + 4 + 5
                  = **12 feet**

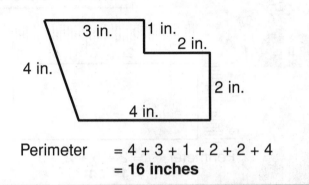

Perimeter   = 4 + 3 + 1 + 2 + 2 + 4
                  = **16 inches**

Find the perimeter of the following objects.

1.

4 yd.

2 yd.   2 yd.

4 yd.

_____ yd.

2.

3 ft.   5 ft.

4 ft.

_____ ft.

3.

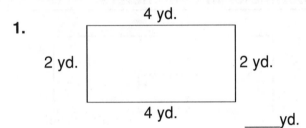

1 ft.

1 ft.

5 ft.

_____ ft.

4.

3 yd.   3 yd.

3 yd.   3 yd.

_____ yd.

5.

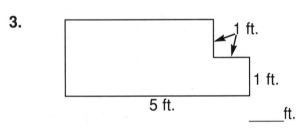

8 in.

6 in.

7 in.

6 in.

8 in.

_____ in.

6.

2 ft.

4 ft.

2 ft.

4 ft.

2 ft.

_____ ft.

7.

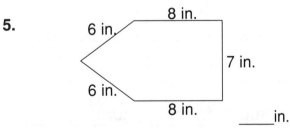

1 yd.   1 yd.

1 yd.   1 yd.

1 yd.

_____ yd.

8.

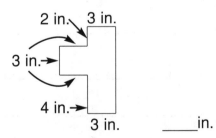

2 in.   3 in.

3 in.

4 in.

3 in.

_____ in.

Math Connection—Grade 5—RBP0172   www.summerbridgeactivities.com   ©RBP Books

Area

This should be a piece of cake for a genius like you!

The **area** of a rectangle is equal to its *length* times its *width*.

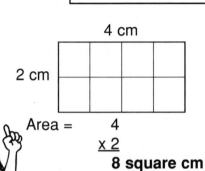

4 cm

2 cm

Area =   4
           x 2
        8 square cm

| length |
| x width |
| area |

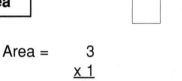

Area =   3
           x 1
        3 square units

Find the area.

1.

4 ft.

3 ft.

_____ square feet

5 m

5 m

_____ square meters

2.

10 km

2 km

_____square kilometers

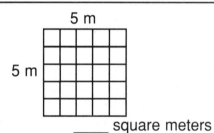

12 in.

7 in.

_____ square inches

Fill in the blanks.

	Length	Width	Area
3.	3 feet	6 feet	_____ square feet
4.	1 inch	4 inches	_____ square inches
5.	5 cm	6 cm	_____ square cm
6.	3 km	5 km	_____ square km
7.	4 mm	_____ mm	__20__ square mm

© RBP Books
www.summerbridgeactivities.com

Math Connection—Grade 5—RBP0172

Pre-Test: Adding and Subtracting Fractions

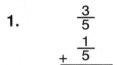

Add.
Simplify if possible.

1. $\dfrac{3}{5}$ $+\dfrac{1}{5}$ $\dfrac{5}{12}$ $+\dfrac{1}{12}$ $\dfrac{4}{5}$ $+\dfrac{4}{5}$ $\dfrac{1}{6}$ $+\dfrac{5}{6}$

2. $2\dfrac{3}{8}$ $+1\dfrac{1}{8}$ $5\dfrac{1}{3}$ $+\dfrac{1}{3}$ $7\dfrac{4}{7}$ $+8\dfrac{5}{7}$ $9\dfrac{5}{12}$ $+3\dfrac{7}{12}$

3. $\dfrac{2}{3}$ $+\dfrac{1}{4}$ $\dfrac{5}{6}$ $+\dfrac{3}{4}$ $2\dfrac{1}{3}$ $+8\dfrac{5}{6}$ $3\dfrac{4}{5}$ $+2\dfrac{1}{2}$

Subtract.
Simplify if possible.

4. $\dfrac{7}{8}$ $-\dfrac{1}{8}$ $2\dfrac{4}{5}$ $-1\dfrac{1}{5}$ $3\dfrac{1}{4}$ $-2\dfrac{3}{4}$ $5\dfrac{9}{12}$ $-3\dfrac{11}{12}$

5. $\dfrac{11}{12}$ $-\dfrac{5}{6}$ $\dfrac{5}{8}$ $-\dfrac{1}{6}$ $7\dfrac{5}{7}$ $-2\dfrac{3}{7}$ $13\dfrac{2}{5}$ $-8\dfrac{8}{15}$

Math Connection—Grade 5—RBP0172   www.summerbridgeactivities.com   © RBP Books

Adding Fractions

 + = numerator → denominator →

$$\frac{1}{3} \quad + \quad \frac{1}{3} \quad = \quad \frac{2}{3}$$

numerator
denominator

Fill in the blanks and color in the blank objects using the information given.

1. + =

$$\frac{1}{2} \quad + \quad \underline{} \quad = \quad \frac{2}{2} \text{ or } 1$$

2.  + =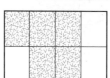

$$\underline{} \quad + \quad \frac{2}{4} \quad = \quad \underline{}$$

3.  + 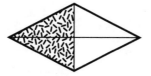 =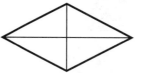

$$\underline{} \quad + \quad \frac{2}{8} \quad = \quad \underline{}$$

4. + =

$$\underline{} \quad + \quad \underline{} \quad = \quad \frac{5}{6}$$

© RBP Books   www.summerbridgeactivities.com   **Math Connection—Grade 5—RBP0172**

Adding Fractions

Add. Simplify if possible.

 $\dfrac{2}{5}$ +
$+\dfrac{1}{5}$
$\overline{}$
$\dfrac{3}{5}$

When adding fractions with like denominators:
1. Add the numerators.
2. Keep the same denominator.
3. Simplify if possible.

$\dfrac{5}{12}$ +
$+\dfrac{5}{12}$
$\overline{}$
$\dfrac{10}{12} = \dfrac{5}{6}$

1. $\dfrac{3}{5}$ $\dfrac{1}{3}$ $\dfrac{1}{6}$ $\dfrac{1}{9}$

$+\dfrac{1}{5}$ $+\dfrac{1}{3}$ $+\dfrac{3}{6}$ $+\dfrac{2}{9}$

2. $\dfrac{1}{7}$ $\dfrac{1}{4}$ $\dfrac{1}{12}$ $\dfrac{3}{10}$

$+\dfrac{2}{7}$ $+\dfrac{1}{4}$ $+\dfrac{4}{12}$ $+\dfrac{4}{10}$

3. $\dfrac{3}{6}$ $\dfrac{1}{11}$ $\dfrac{3}{8}$ $\dfrac{4}{9}$

$+\dfrac{2}{6}$ $+\dfrac{3}{11}$ $+\dfrac{3}{8}$ $+\dfrac{3}{9}$

4. $\dfrac{2}{9}$ $\dfrac{3}{12}$ $\dfrac{5}{11}$ $\dfrac{5}{8}$

$+\dfrac{2}{9}$ $+\dfrac{5}{12}$ $+\dfrac{2}{11}$ $+\dfrac{2}{8}$

Math Connection—Grade 5—RBP0172   www.summerbridgeactivities.com   © RBP Books

Adding Fractions

Add. Then simplify.

$$\begin{array}{r} \frac{3}{7} \\ \frac{6}{7} \\ + \hline \\ \frac{9}{7} = 1\frac{2}{7} \end{array}$$

Add.

Simplify.

$$\begin{array}{r} \frac{7}{8} \\ \frac{5}{8} \\ + \hline \\ \frac{12}{8} = 1\frac{4}{8} = 1\frac{1}{2} \end{array}$$

1.
$$\begin{array}{r} \frac{2}{6} \\ \frac{4}{6} \\ + \hline \end{array}$$
$$\begin{array}{r} \frac{2}{3} \\ \frac{2}{3} \\ + \hline \end{array}$$
$$\begin{array}{r} \frac{6}{7} \\ \frac{2}{7} \\ + \hline \end{array}$$
$$\begin{array}{r} \frac{3}{10} \\ \frac{2}{10} \\ + \hline \end{array}$$

2.
$$\begin{array}{r} \frac{2}{5} \\ \frac{4}{5} \\ + \hline \end{array}$$
$$\begin{array}{r} \frac{5}{12} \\ \frac{1}{12} \\ + \hline \end{array}$$
$$\begin{array}{r} \frac{1}{2} \\ \frac{1}{2} \\ + \hline \end{array}$$
$$\begin{array}{r} \frac{4}{6} \\ \frac{5}{6} \\ + \hline \end{array}$$

3.
$$\begin{array}{r} \frac{4}{7} \\ \frac{5}{7} \\ + \hline \end{array}$$
$$\begin{array}{r} \frac{3}{8} \\ \frac{2}{8} \\ + \hline \end{array}$$
$$\begin{array}{r} \frac{5}{6} \\ \frac{5}{6} \\ + \hline \end{array}$$
$$\begin{array}{r} \frac{2}{9} \\ \frac{4}{9} \\ + \hline \end{array}$$

4.
$$\begin{array}{r} \frac{7}{10} \\ \frac{5}{10} \\ + \hline \end{array}$$
$$\begin{array}{r} \frac{3}{4} \\ \frac{3}{4} \\ + \hline \end{array}$$
$$\begin{array}{r} \frac{7}{8} \\ \frac{3}{8} \\ + \hline \end{array}$$
$$\begin{array}{r} \frac{7}{12} \\ \frac{9}{12} \\ + \hline \end{array}$$

© RBP Books   www.summerbridgeactivities.com   **Math Connection—Grade 5—RBP0172**

Adding Mixed Numbers

Add. Simplify if possible.

$3\frac{2}{6}$	Add the fractions.	$2\frac{5}{12}$	
$+\ 2\frac{1}{6}$	Add the whole numbers.	$+\ 1\frac{11}{12}$	
$5\frac{3}{6} = 5\frac{1}{2}$	Simplify if possible.	$3\frac{16}{12} = 3 + 1 + \frac{4}{12} = 4\frac{1}{3}$	

1.

$3\frac{1}{3}$
$+\ 2\frac{1}{3}$

$4\frac{2}{5}$
$+\ \frac{1}{5}$

$3\frac{3}{8}$
$+\ 2\frac{5}{8}$

$7\frac{3}{4}$
$+\ 5\frac{3}{4}$

2.

$2\frac{4}{5}$
$+\ 3\frac{2}{5}$

$13\frac{5}{8}$
$+\ \frac{7}{8}$

$1\frac{3}{4}$
$+\ 2\frac{3}{4}$

$4\frac{1}{7}$
$+\ 2\frac{2}{7}$

3.

$10\frac{2}{9}$
$+\ 2\frac{7}{9}$

$3\frac{5}{6}$
$+\ 2\frac{3}{6}$

$2\frac{7}{10}$
$+\ 1\frac{4}{10}$

$3\frac{3}{5}$
$+\ 1\frac{1}{5}$

4.

$5\frac{4}{8}$
$+\ \frac{2}{8}$

$3\frac{7}{12}$
$+\ 4\frac{9}{12}$

$8\frac{7}{9}$
$+\ 9\frac{5}{9}$

$23\frac{4}{10}$
$+\ 17\frac{7}{10}$

Math Connection—Grade 5—RBP0172   www.summerbridgeactivities.com   ©RBP Books

Adding Fractions

Add. Simplify if possible.

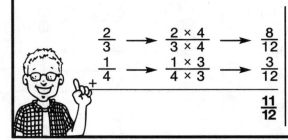

When adding fractions with unlike denominators:

$\dfrac{2}{3} \rightarrow \dfrac{2 \times 4}{3 \times 4} \rightarrow \dfrac{8}{12}$

$\dfrac{1}{4} \rightarrow \dfrac{1 \times 3}{4 \times 3} \rightarrow \dfrac{3}{12}$

$+ \hspace{2cm} \dfrac{11}{12}$

1. Find the least common denominator (LCD).
2. Rewrite each fraction using the LCD.
3. Add.
4. Simplify if possible.

$\dfrac{5}{6} \rightarrow \dfrac{5 \times 5}{6 \times 5} \rightarrow \dfrac{25}{30}$

$\dfrac{2}{5} \rightarrow \dfrac{2 \times 6}{5 \times 6} \rightarrow \dfrac{12}{30}$

$+ \hspace{2cm} \dfrac{37}{30}$

$= 1\dfrac{7}{30}$

1. $\dfrac{2}{5}$ $\dfrac{3}{8}$ $\dfrac{1}{2}$ $\dfrac{3}{4}$

    $+ \dfrac{1}{3}$ $+ \dfrac{1}{3}$ $+ \dfrac{1}{3}$ $+ \dfrac{3}{5}$

2. $\dfrac{5}{6}$ $\dfrac{2}{7}$ $\dfrac{3}{10}$ $\dfrac{5}{9}$

    $+ \dfrac{2}{5}$ $+ \dfrac{2}{3}$ $+ \dfrac{1}{3}$ $+ \dfrac{1}{2}$

3. $\dfrac{3}{4}$ $\dfrac{1}{3}$ $\dfrac{1}{3}$ $\dfrac{7}{10}$

    $+ \dfrac{1}{7}$ $+ \dfrac{5}{8}$ $+ \dfrac{3}{4}$ $+ \dfrac{2}{3}$

© RBP Books   www.summerbridgeactivities.com   Math Connection—Grade 5—RBP0172

Adding Fractions

Add. Simplify if possible.

When adding fractions with unlike denominators:

$$\frac{1}{6} \longrightarrow \frac{1}{6}$$
$$\frac{2}{3} \longrightarrow \frac{2 \times 2}{3 \times 2} \longrightarrow \frac{4}{6}$$
$$+ \underline{}$$
$$\frac{5}{6}$$

1. Find the least common denominator.
2. Rewrite each fraction using the LCD.
3. Add.
4. Simplify if possible.

$$\frac{5}{6} \longrightarrow \frac{5 \times 2}{6 \times 2} \longrightarrow \frac{10}{12}$$
$$\frac{7}{12} \longrightarrow \frac{7}{12}$$
$$+ \underline{}$$
$$\frac{17}{12}$$
$$= 1\frac{5}{12}$$

1.

$$\frac{2}{3}$$
$$+\frac{4}{9}$$

$$\frac{1}{4}$$
$$+\frac{5}{8}$$

$$\frac{3}{5}$$
$$+\frac{1}{10}$$

$$\frac{5}{8}$$
$$+\frac{1}{2}$$

2.

$$\frac{1}{3}$$
$$+\frac{5}{6}$$

$$\frac{1}{5}$$
$$+\frac{4}{15}$$

$$\frac{1}{6}$$
$$+\frac{2}{3}$$

$$\frac{7}{8}$$
$$+\frac{3}{4}$$

3.

$$\frac{1}{2}$$
$$+\frac{7}{8}$$

$$\frac{5}{8}$$
$$+\frac{1}{4}$$

$$\frac{6}{7}$$
$$+\frac{1}{14}$$

$$\frac{5}{12}$$
$$+\frac{5}{6}$$

Math Connection—Grade 5—RBP0172   www.summerbridgeactivities.com   ©RBP Books

Adding Fractions
Add. Simplify if possible.

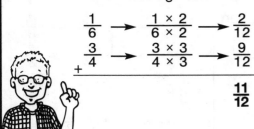

When adding fractions with unlike denominators:

$$\frac{1}{6} \rightarrow \frac{1 \times 2}{6 \times 2} \rightarrow \frac{2}{12}$$

$$+ \frac{3}{4} \rightarrow \frac{3 \times 3}{4 \times 3} \rightarrow \frac{9}{12}$$

$$\frac{11}{12}$$

1. Find the least common denominator.
2. Rewrite each fraction using the LCD.
3. Add.
4. Simplify if possible.

$$\frac{5}{6} \rightarrow \frac{5 \times 4}{6 \times 4} \rightarrow \frac{20}{24}$$

$$+ \frac{5}{8} \rightarrow \frac{5 \times 3}{8 \times 3} \rightarrow \frac{15}{24}$$

$$\frac{35}{24}$$

$$= 1\frac{11}{24}$$

1.
$$\frac{1}{6}$$
$$+ \frac{1}{4}$$

$$\frac{5}{8}$$
$$+ \frac{1}{6}$$

$$\frac{3}{4}$$
$$+ \frac{5}{6}$$

$$\frac{1}{6}$$
$$+ \frac{7}{10}$$

2.
$$\frac{5}{9}$$
$$+ \frac{4}{6}$$

$$\frac{3}{10}$$
$$+ \frac{1}{6}$$

$$\frac{3}{4}$$
$$+ \frac{3}{10}$$

$$\frac{5}{6}$$
$$+ \frac{7}{8}$$

3.
$$\frac{5}{6}$$
$$+ \frac{3}{10}$$

$$\frac{4}{9}$$
$$+ \frac{1}{6}$$

$$\frac{3}{8}$$
$$+ \frac{5}{12}$$

$$\frac{5}{8}$$
$$+ \frac{9}{10}$$

© RBP Books   www.summerbridgeactivities.com   Math Connection—Grade 5—RBP0172

Adding Mixed Numbers

Add. Simplify if possible.

When adding fractions with unlike denominators:

$$2\frac{1}{3} \rightarrow \frac{1 \times 4}{3 \times 4} \rightarrow \frac{4}{12}$$

$$3\frac{3}{4} \rightarrow \frac{3 \times 3}{4 \times 3} \rightarrow \frac{9}{12}$$

$$+ \qquad\qquad\qquad\qquad$$

$$5 \qquad\qquad\qquad\qquad \frac{13}{12}$$

$$= 5 + 1\frac{1}{12} = \mathbf{6\frac{1}{12}}$$

1. Find the Least Common Denominator.
2. Rewrite each fraction using the LCD.
3. Add.
4. Simplify if possible.

$$1\frac{7}{8} \longrightarrow \frac{7}{8}$$

$$2\frac{1}{4} \rightarrow \frac{1 \times 2}{4 \times 2} \rightarrow \frac{2}{8}$$

$$+ \qquad\qquad\qquad\qquad$$

$$3 \qquad\qquad\qquad\qquad \frac{9}{8}$$

$$= 3 + 1\frac{1}{8} = \mathbf{4\frac{1}{8}}$$

1.

$1\frac{3}{8}$ $\qquad$ $2\frac{3}{4}$ $\qquad$ $5\frac{1}{3}$ $\qquad$ $3\frac{2}{3}$

$+\ 4\frac{1}{6}$ $\qquad$ $+\ 3\frac{1}{5}$ $\qquad$ $+\ 1\frac{5}{6}$ $\qquad$ $+\ 2\frac{1}{4}$

2.

$6\frac{1}{2}$ $\qquad$ $5\frac{2}{5}$ $\qquad$ $4\frac{1}{6}$ $\qquad$ $1\frac{7}{8}$

$+\ \ \frac{3}{4}$ $\qquad$ $+\ 2\frac{1}{3}$ $\qquad$ $+\ 2\frac{3}{4}$ $\qquad$ $+\ 2\frac{1}{6}$

3.

$4\frac{5}{12}$ $\qquad$ $1\frac{2}{5}$ $\qquad$ $2\frac{3}{8}$ $\qquad$ $6\frac{7}{11}$

$+\ 2\frac{5}{6}$ $\qquad$ $+\ 3\frac{7}{10}$ $\qquad$ $+\ 7\frac{1}{2}$ $\qquad$ $+\ 5\frac{1}{2}$

Adding Fractions
Add. Simplify if possible.

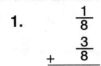

1.
$\dfrac{1}{8}$
$+ \dfrac{3}{8}$

$\dfrac{5}{12}$
$+ \dfrac{1}{12}$

$\dfrac{1}{5}$
$+ \dfrac{1}{5}$

$\dfrac{8}{9}$
$+ \dfrac{4}{9}$

2.
$2\dfrac{1}{3}$
$+ \dfrac{1}{3}$

$3\dfrac{1}{4}$
$5\dfrac{3}{4}$
$+$

$\dfrac{5}{6}$
$2\dfrac{1}{6}$
$+$

$4\dfrac{2}{9}$
$5\dfrac{1}{9}$
$+$

3.
3
$+ \dfrac{2}{7}$

5
$+ \dfrac{1}{7}$

5
$+ \dfrac{9}{11}$

$\dfrac{5}{6}$
$+ \dfrac{1}{3}$

4.
$\dfrac{5}{8}$
$+ \dfrac{5}{6}$

$\dfrac{3}{4}$
$+ \dfrac{1}{5}$

$\dfrac{1}{5}$
$+ \dfrac{6}{15}$

$\dfrac{1}{8}$
$+ \dfrac{5}{12}$

5.
$5\dfrac{5}{6}$
$2\dfrac{1}{3}$
$+$

$5\dfrac{1}{3}$
$2\dfrac{1}{8}$
$+$

$4\dfrac{1}{9}$
$2\dfrac{1}{6}$
$+$

$1\dfrac{1}{5}$
$3\dfrac{3}{10}$
$+$

© RBP Books
www.summerbridgeactivities.com

Math Connection—Grade 5—RBP0172

Subtracting Fractions

Subtract. Simplify if possible.

To subtract fractions with like denominators:

$$\frac{2}{5}$$
$$-\frac{1}{5}$$
$$\overline{\frac{1}{5}}$$

1. Subtract the numerators.
2. Keep the same denominator.
3. Simplify if possible.

$$\frac{7}{8}$$
$$-\frac{3}{8}$$
$$\overline{\frac{4}{8}} = \frac{1}{2}$$

1. $\frac{3}{8}$ $\frac{7}{12}$ $\frac{5}{6}$ $\frac{6}{7}$
   $-\frac{1}{8}$ $-\frac{5}{12}$ $-\frac{1}{6}$ $-\frac{3}{7}$

2. $\frac{11}{12}$ $\frac{9}{10}$ $\frac{4}{5}$ $\frac{2}{3}$
   $-\frac{1}{12}$ $-\frac{3}{10}$ $-\frac{2}{5}$ $-\frac{1}{3}$

3. $\frac{3}{4}$ $\frac{11}{12}$ $\frac{10}{11}$ $\frac{13}{16}$
   $-\frac{1}{4}$ $-\frac{5}{12}$ $-\frac{3}{11}$ $-\frac{3}{16}$

© RBP Books   www.summerbridgeactivities.com   Math Connection—Grade 5—RBP0172

Subtracting Fractions

Subtract.

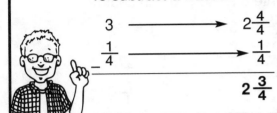

To subtract a fraction from a whole number:

$3 \longrightarrow 2\frac{4}{4}$

$-\frac{1}{4} \longrightarrow \frac{1}{4}$

$2\frac{3}{4}$

1. Rewrite the whole number as an equivalent fraction using the LCD.
2. Subtract.

$2 \longrightarrow 1\frac{6}{6}$

$-\frac{5}{6} \longrightarrow \frac{5}{6}$

$1\frac{1}{6}$

1.

5
$-\frac{7}{8}$

3
$-\frac{1}{3}$

6
$-\frac{7}{9}$

4
$-\frac{2}{5}$

2.

8
$-\frac{4}{5}$

5
$-\frac{4}{9}$

12
$-\frac{3}{11}$

9
$-\frac{8}{9}$

3.

7
$-\frac{1}{3}$

10
$-\frac{1}{5}$

12
$-\frac{7}{10}$

8
$-\frac{5}{6}$

Math Connection—Grade 5—RBP0172 www.summerbridgeactivities.com ©RBP Books

Subtracting Mixed Numbers
Subtract. Simplify if possible.

Rewrite $3\frac{1}{4}$ so you can subtract.

$$3\frac{1}{4} = 2 + 1\frac{1}{4} = 2\frac{5}{4}$$
$$1\frac{3}{4} \longrightarrow 1\frac{3}{4}$$
$$\overline{}\quad 1\frac{2}{4} = 1\frac{1}{2}$$

Rewrite $6\frac{2}{9}$ so you can subtract.

$$6\frac{2}{9} = 5 + 1\frac{2}{9} = 5\frac{11}{9}$$
$$5\frac{4}{9} \longrightarrow 5\frac{4}{9}$$
$$\overline{}\quad \frac{7}{9}$$

1. $3\frac{3}{7}$ $5\frac{1}{3}$ $4\frac{1}{6}$ $8\frac{3}{8}$
   $-\,1\frac{5}{7}$ $-\,2\frac{2}{3}$ $-\,3\frac{5}{6}$ $-\,2\frac{5}{8}$

2. $6\frac{1}{5}$ $4\frac{3}{10}$ $8\frac{2}{5}$ $10\frac{5}{12}$
   $-\,3\frac{3}{5}$ $-\,3\frac{7}{10}$ $-\,5\frac{4}{5}$ $-\,7\frac{7}{12}$

3. $3\frac{1}{8}$ $6\frac{4}{9}$ $12\frac{5}{12}$ $9\frac{1}{4}$
   $-\,2\frac{5}{8}$ $-\,5\frac{7}{9}$ $-\,10\frac{7}{12}$ $-\,3\frac{3}{4}$

© RBP Books   www.summerbridgeactivities.com   Math Connection—Grade 5—RBP0172

Subtracting Mixed Numbers
Subtract. Simplify if possible.

1. $5\frac{1}{4}$ $7\frac{3}{7}$ $8\frac{5}{12}$ $4\frac{3}{8}$
   $-\,2\frac{3}{4}$ $-\,5\frac{4}{7}$ $-\,7\frac{11}{12}$ $-\,2\frac{5}{8}$

2. $10\frac{1}{7}$ $8\frac{3}{10}$ $5\frac{2}{5}$ $6\frac{1}{6}$
   $-\,9\frac{6}{7}$ $-\,5\frac{7}{10}$ $-\,1\frac{4}{5}$ $-\,2\frac{5}{6}$

3. $2\frac{6}{11}$ $5\frac{1}{3}$ $7\frac{1}{5}$ $10\frac{2}{10}$
   $-\,\frac{8}{11}$ $-\,4\frac{2}{3}$ $-\,4\frac{2}{5}$ $-\,9\frac{7}{10}$

4. $6\frac{2}{6}$ $8\frac{3}{7}$ $7\frac{1}{4}$ $12\frac{1}{3}$
   $-\,1\frac{5}{6}$ $-\,2\frac{5}{7}$ $-\,2\frac{3}{4}$ $-\,2\frac{2}{3}$

5. $2\frac{2}{12}$ $8\frac{3}{10}$ $5\frac{1}{8}$ $12\frac{1}{6}$
   $-\,1\frac{11}{12}$ $-\,3\frac{7}{10}$ $-\,2\frac{7}{8}$ $-\,4\frac{5}{6}$

www.summerbridgeactivities.com   © RBP Books

Subtracting Fractions

Subtract. Simplify if possible.

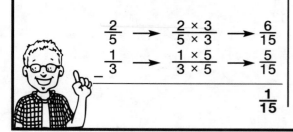

To subtract fractions with unlike denominators:

$$\frac{2}{5} \rightarrow \frac{2 \times 3}{5 \times 3} \rightarrow \frac{6}{15}$$

$$\frac{1}{3} \rightarrow \frac{1 \times 5}{3 \times 5} \rightarrow \frac{5}{15}$$

$$-\ \frac{1}{15}$$

1. Find the LCD.

2. Rewrite using LCD.

3. Subtract.

$$\frac{5}{8} \rightarrow \frac{5 \times 3}{8 \times 3} \rightarrow \frac{15}{24}$$

$$\frac{1}{3} \rightarrow \frac{1 \times 8}{3 \times 8} \rightarrow \frac{8}{24}$$

$$-\ \frac{7}{24}$$

1. $\frac{2}{3}$ $\frac{4}{5}$ $\frac{1}{2}$ $\frac{5}{7}$

$-\ \frac{1}{4}$ $-\ \frac{1}{2}$ $-\ \frac{1}{3}$ $-\ \frac{1}{2}$

2. $\frac{1}{2}$ $\frac{2}{3}$ $\frac{3}{4}$ $\frac{4}{5}$

$-\ \frac{2}{9}$ $-\ \frac{2}{7}$ $-\ \frac{1}{5}$ $-\ \frac{2}{7}$

3. $\frac{3}{5}$ $\frac{7}{8}$ $\frac{5}{6}$ $\frac{9}{11}$

$-\ \frac{2}{9}$ $-\ \frac{2}{5}$ $-\ \frac{1}{7}$ $-\ \frac{1}{6}$

© RBP Books   www.summerbridgeactivities.com   Math Connection—Grade 5—RBP0172

Subtracting Fractions

Subtract. Simplify if possible.

To subtract fractions with unlike denominators:

$$\frac{3}{4} \rightarrow \frac{3 \times 3}{4 \times 3} \rightarrow \frac{9}{12}$$
$$\frac{1}{6} \rightarrow \frac{1 \times 2}{6 \times 2} \rightarrow \frac{2}{12}$$
$$\overline{} \qquad \qquad \frac{7}{12}$$

1. Find the LCD.
2. Rewrite fractions using the LCD.
3. Subtract.
4. Simplify if possible.

$$\frac{7}{12} \rightarrow \qquad \rightarrow \frac{7}{12}$$
$$\frac{1}{4} \rightarrow \frac{1 \times 3}{4 \times 3} \rightarrow \frac{3}{12}$$
$$\overline{} \qquad \frac{4}{12} = \frac{1}{3}$$

1.
$$\begin{array}{r} \frac{3}{4} \\ -\ \frac{7}{10} \\ \hline \end{array}$$
$$\begin{array}{r} \frac{7}{9} \\ -\ \frac{1}{6} \\ \hline \end{array}$$
$$\begin{array}{r} \frac{1}{2} \\ -\ \frac{3}{8} \\ \hline \end{array}$$
$$\begin{array}{r} \frac{2}{3} \\ -\ \frac{2}{9} \\ \hline \end{array}$$

2.
$$\begin{array}{r} \frac{7}{12} \\ -\ \frac{1}{4} \\ \hline \end{array}$$
$$\begin{array}{r} \frac{7}{10} \\ -\ \frac{1}{2} \\ \hline \end{array}$$
$$\begin{array}{r} \frac{3}{4} \\ -\ \frac{3}{8} \\ \hline \end{array}$$
$$\begin{array}{r} \frac{3}{10} \\ -\ \frac{1}{5} \\ \hline \end{array}$$

3.
$$\begin{array}{r} \frac{5}{8} \\ -\ \frac{1}{6} \\ \hline \end{array}$$
$$\begin{array}{r} \frac{5}{6} \\ -\ \frac{3}{10} \\ \hline \end{array}$$
$$\begin{array}{r} \frac{3}{4} \\ -\ \frac{1}{6} \\ \hline \end{array}$$
$$\begin{array}{r} \frac{7}{8} \\ -\ \frac{5}{6} \\ \hline \end{array}$$

Subtracting Fractions
Subtract. Simplify if possible.

1.
$$-\frac{\frac{1}{2}}{\frac{1}{3}}$$
$$-\frac{\frac{4}{5}}{\frac{1}{6}}$$
$$-\frac{\frac{3}{4}}{\frac{1}{6}}$$
$$-\frac{\frac{3}{5}}{\frac{1}{2}}$$

2.
$$-\frac{\frac{3}{4}}{\frac{3}{8}}$$
$$-\frac{\frac{1}{2}}{\frac{3}{10}}$$
$$-\frac{\frac{1}{2}}{\frac{1}{4}}$$
$$-\frac{\frac{7}{8}}{\frac{1}{2}}$$

3.
$$-\frac{\frac{5}{8}}{\frac{1}{3}}$$
$$-\frac{\frac{4}{5}}{\frac{3}{10}}$$
$$-\frac{\frac{2}{3}}{\frac{2}{9}}$$
$$-\frac{\frac{5}{6}}{\frac{4}{9}}$$

4.
$$-\frac{\frac{5}{8}}{\frac{1}{6}}$$
$$-\frac{\frac{11}{12}}{\frac{3}{4}}$$
$$-\frac{\frac{2}{3}}{\frac{1}{4}}$$
$$-\frac{\frac{5}{6}}{\frac{1}{2}}$$

5.
$$-\frac{\frac{2}{3}}{\frac{1}{6}}$$
$$-\frac{\frac{3}{4}}{\frac{2}{5}}$$
$$-\frac{\frac{5}{12}}{\frac{1}{3}}$$
$$-\frac{\frac{4}{5}}{\frac{2}{3}}$$

© RBP Books   www.summerbridgeactivities.com   Math Connection—Grade 5—RBP0172

Subtracting Mixed Numbers

Subtract. Simplify if possible.

Steps 1 & 2   Step 3

$8\frac{1}{3} \longrightarrow 8\frac{8}{24} \longrightarrow 7\frac{32}{24}$

$6\frac{5}{8} \longrightarrow 6\frac{15}{24} \longrightarrow 6\frac{15}{24}$

$1\frac{17}{24}$

Step 3

$8\frac{8}{24} = 7 + 1 + \frac{8}{24}$

$= 7 + \frac{24}{24} + \frac{8}{24}$

$= 7 + \frac{32}{24}$

Steps for Subtracting Mixed Numbers:
1. Find the LCD.
2. Rewrite the fraction(s) using the LCD.
3. Rewrite again, if needed, to subtract.
4. Subtract.
5. Simplify if possible.

1.
$4\frac{1}{3}$
$-\ 2\frac{1}{2}$

$6\frac{1}{8}$
$-\ 5\frac{1}{6}$

$5\frac{1}{4}$
$-\ 3\frac{1}{2}$

$8\frac{3}{5}$
$-\ 5\frac{1}{3}$

2.
$6\frac{3}{8}$
$-\ 5\frac{3}{4}$

$4\frac{2}{9}$
$-\ 3\frac{2}{3}$

$9\frac{1}{6}$
$-\ 7\frac{1}{3}$

$5\frac{2}{5}$
$-\ 3\frac{7}{10}$

3.
$6\frac{1}{3}$
$-\ 4\frac{5}{8}$

$7\frac{1}{4}$
$-\ 3\frac{7}{8}$

$9\frac{3}{10}$
$-\ 5\frac{4}{5}$

$3\frac{5}{12}$
$-\ 2\frac{2}{3}$

www.summerbridgeactivities.com   © RBP Books

Subtracting Fractions

Subtract. Simplify if possible.

1.
$$\frac{3}{4} - \frac{1}{4}$$
$$\frac{6}{7} - \frac{2}{3}$$
$$5\frac{1}{3} - 2\frac{2}{3}$$
$$6 - \frac{7}{8}$$

2.
$$\frac{4}{5} - \frac{1}{2}$$
$$\frac{3}{8} - \frac{1}{4}$$
$$2\frac{5}{6} - \frac{1}{3}$$
$$7\frac{7}{8} - \frac{3}{8}$$

3.
$$\frac{5}{12} - \frac{1}{12}$$
$$8\frac{7}{8} - 2\frac{3}{8}$$
$$9\frac{3}{4} - 3\frac{1}{3}$$
$$2\frac{1}{3} - \frac{4}{5}$$

4.
$$11\frac{3}{5} - 2\frac{1}{5}$$
$$4\frac{4}{5} - \frac{8}{10}$$
$$\frac{7}{11} - \frac{1}{3}$$
$$\frac{5}{8} - \frac{4}{12}$$

5.
$$9\frac{2}{3} - \frac{2}{3}$$
$$\frac{7}{12} - \frac{5}{12}$$
$$2 - \frac{5}{6}$$
$$10\frac{3}{8} - 9\frac{3}{4}$$

©RBP Books

Subtracting Fractions

Subtract. Simplify if possible.

1. $\quad 4\frac{2}{3}$ $\qquad\qquad$ $\frac{3}{8}$ $\qquad\qquad$ $6\frac{3}{8}$ $\qquad\qquad$ $\frac{5}{12}$

$\quad -\ 2\frac{1}{3}$ $\qquad\quad -\ \frac{1}{4}$ $\qquad\quad -\ 2\frac{1}{3}$ $\qquad\quad -\ \frac{1}{12}$

2. $\quad 5\frac{5}{7}$ $\qquad\qquad$ $\frac{11}{12}$ $\qquad\qquad$ $6\frac{1}{3}$ $\qquad\qquad$ $\frac{7}{12}$

$\quad -\ 2\frac{1}{2}$ $\qquad\quad -\ \frac{3}{4}$ $\qquad\quad -\ 5\frac{5}{6}$ $\qquad\quad -\ \frac{3}{8}$

3. $\quad 7$ $\qquad\qquad\quad$ $6\frac{1}{3}$ $\qquad\qquad$ $6\frac{7}{8}$ $\qquad\qquad$ $\frac{3}{4}$

$\quad -\ \frac{5}{8}$ $\qquad\quad -\ 2\frac{2}{5}$ $\qquad\quad -\ 4\frac{5}{6}$ $\qquad\quad -\ \frac{1}{3}$

4. $\quad 3\frac{7}{12}$ $\qquad\qquad$ $\frac{7}{11}$ $\qquad\qquad$ 6 $\qquad\qquad\quad$ $5\frac{1}{5}$

$\quad -\ \frac{5}{12}$ $\qquad\quad -\ \frac{3}{11}$ $\qquad\quad -\ \frac{1}{3}$ $\qquad\quad -\ 2\frac{3}{10}$

5. $\quad \frac{3}{8}$ $\qquad\qquad\quad$ $7\frac{8}{9}$ $\qquad\qquad$ $\frac{5}{6}$ $\qquad\qquad\quad$ $9\frac{1}{6}$

$\quad -\ \frac{1}{8}$ $\qquad\quad -\ 4\frac{4}{9}$ $\qquad\quad -\ \frac{1}{8}$ $\qquad\quad -\ 2\frac{3}{4}$

©RBP Books
www.summerbridgeactivities.com $\qquad\qquad$ Math Connection—Grade 5—RBP0172

Problem Solving

Four classmates, Rachel, Grant, Ethan, and Sarah, are competing in an obstacle course. The course is one mile long. Each person must complete one part of the competition. The course begins with running through tires for $\frac{1}{6}$ mile, dribbling a basketball for $\frac{1}{4}$ mile, running $\frac{1}{2}$ mile, and then crossing the monkey bars.

1. If Rachel runs through the tires for $\frac{1}{6}$ of a mile and Grant dribbles the basketball for $\frac{1}{4}$ mile, what fraction of the course have Rachel and Grant completed?

2. **a.** If Ethan then runs for $\frac{1}{2}$ mile, how much of the course have Rachel, Grant, and Ethan completed?

   b. What fraction of the one-mile course must Sarah cross on the monkey bars?

3. **a.** What fraction of the course did the boys, Grant and Ethan, cover?

   b. What fraction did the girls, Rachel and Sarah, cover?

4. It took the team 25 minutes to complete the race. If it took Rachel $5\frac{1}{4}$ minutes, Grant $7\frac{1}{4}$ minutes, and Sarah $6\frac{1}{6}$ minutes, how long did it take Ethan to run the $\frac{1}{2}$ mile?

Problem Solving

Leave answers as fractions. Simplify if possible.

Jobs	Tanya's Time per Job	Tyrell's Time per Job
Homework	$2\frac{1}{4}$ hours	$1\frac{2}{3}$ hours
Clean bathroom	$\frac{3}{4}$ hour	$\frac{1}{2}$ hour
Clean bedroom	$\frac{1}{3}$ hour	1 hour
Walk dog	$\frac{1}{2}$ hour	$\frac{3}{4}$ hour

1. How much total time does it take both Tanya and Tyrell to do their homework?

2. How much more time does Tanya spend on her homework than Tyrell?

3. How much more time does Tyrell spend cleaning his bedroom than Tanya?

4. If Tyrell comes home from school, does his homework, and then walks the dog, how much time will it take him?

5. If Tanya cleans only once a week, how much time does she spend cleaning the bathroom and bedroom?

6. If Tyrell cleans the bathroom two times a week and Tanya cleans the bathroom only once a week, who spends more time cleaning the bathroom?

© RBP Books   www.summerbridgeactivities.com   Math Connection—Grade 5—RBP0172

Post-Test: Adding and Subtracting Fractions

Add.

Simplify if possible.

1.
$$\frac{3}{7} \atop +\frac{1}{7}$$
$$\frac{7}{12} \atop +\frac{5}{12}$$
$$\frac{4}{9} \atop +\frac{2}{9}$$
$$\frac{5}{6} \atop +\frac{5}{6}$$

2.
$$2\frac{3}{10} \atop +1\frac{1}{10}$$
$$8\frac{1}{3} \atop +\frac{2}{3}$$
$$2\frac{3}{8} \atop +8\frac{5}{8}$$
$$1\frac{5}{12} \atop +3\frac{1}{12}$$

3.
$$\frac{2}{3} \atop +\frac{1}{8}$$
$$\frac{1}{6} \atop +\frac{3}{4}$$
$$3\frac{2}{3} \atop +8\frac{1}{6}$$
$$4\frac{4}{5} \atop +1\frac{1}{3}$$

Subtract.

Simplify if possible.

4.
$$\frac{5}{8} \atop -\frac{1}{8}$$
$$4\frac{4}{5} \atop -1\frac{2}{5}$$
$$5\frac{1}{4} \atop -3\frac{3}{4}$$
$$7\frac{3}{12} \atop -3\frac{7}{12}$$

5.
$$\frac{2}{3} \atop -\frac{1}{6}$$
$$\frac{11}{12} \atop -\frac{5}{6}$$
$$7 \atop -\frac{3}{7}$$
$$21\frac{2}{15} \atop -8\frac{4}{5}$$

Probability

Probability is the chance of an event occurring.

The probability of an event can be described as **likely**, **unlikely**, **certain,** or **impossible**.

Suppose we fill up a sack with 10 marbles. One is green and 9 are red.

Is the probability of pulling out a green marble likely, unlikely, certain, or impossible?

The probability of pulling out a green marble is **unlikely**.

Is the probability of pulling out a red marble likely, unlikely, certain, or impossible?

The probability of pulling out a red marble is **likely**.

Is the probability of pulling out a yellow marble likely, unlikely, certain, or impossible?

The probability of pulling out a yellow marble is **impossible**.

Look at the spinner to answer the following questions.

Circle the best answer.

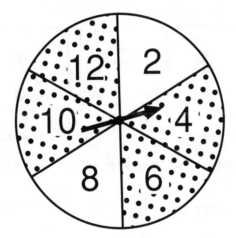

1. The probability of spinning an even number is   likely unlikely certain impossible

2. The probability of spinning a odd number is   likely unlikely certain impossible

3. The probability of landing on a polka-dotted space is   likely unlikely certain impossible

4. The probability of landing on a number greater than 8 is   likely unlikely certain impossible

5. The probability of landing on a 2 is   likely unlikely certain impossible

©RBP Books   www.summerbridgeactivities.com   Math Connection—Grade 5—RBP0172

Probability

Probability can be written as a fraction.

Look at the spinner to the right.

What is the probability of landing on a striped space?

$\frac{2}{8} = \frac{1}{4}$

What is the probability of landing on an even number?

$\frac{4}{8} = \frac{1}{2}$

What is the probability of landing on 12?

$\frac{0}{8} = 0$

What is the probability of landing on a number less than 10?

$\frac{8}{8} = 1$

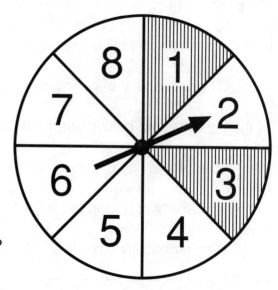

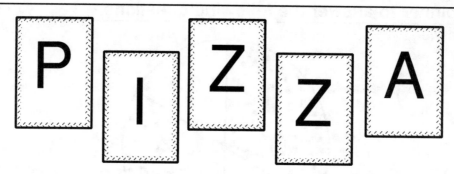

Imagine if we turned the above cards over, mixed them up, and then picked one card. Answer the following questions by writing a fraction.

1. What is the probability of picking a P?

2. What is the probability of picking a Z?

3. What is the probability of picking an E?

4. What is the probability of picking a number?

5. What is the probability of picking any letter?

6. What is the probability of picking a vowel?

Probability

Maria's mother keeps a box full of mismatched socks. In the box there are 5 white, 4 blue, 1 red, 1 gray, and 3 black socks.

What is the probability of pulling out a blue sock?

The probability would equal the number of blue socks over the total number of socks.

$$\frac{Blue}{Total} = \frac{4}{5 + 4 + 1 + 1 + 3} = \frac{4}{14} = \frac{2}{7}$$

What is the probability of pulling out a red sock?

$$\frac{Red}{Total} = \frac{1}{14}$$

Holly bought a bag of candy that had the following colors: 14 brown, 8 yellow, 2 blue, and 6 red. Without looking she pulled out one candy.

1. What is the probability that it is yellow?

2. What is the probability that it is red?

3. What is the probability that it is purple?

4. What is the probability that it is brown?

Raymond has a fruit basket on the kitchen table. It contains 4 green apples, 5 red apples, and 6 oranges. He grabs one piece of fruit.

5. What is the probability that it is red?

6. What is the probability that it is a fruit?

7. What is the probability that it is orange?

8. What is the probability that it is an apple?

© RBP Books   www.summerbridgeactivities.com   Math Connection—Grade 5—RBP0172

Pre-Test: Multiplying Fractions

1. $\frac{2}{3} \times \frac{1}{7} =$ $\frac{1}{4} \times \frac{3}{5} =$ $\frac{4}{5} \times \frac{1}{3} =$ $\frac{4}{11} \times \frac{2}{3} =$

2. $\frac{2}{3} \times \frac{6}{7} =$ $\frac{1}{2} \times \frac{6}{11} =$ $\frac{4}{7} \times \frac{5}{6} =$ $\frac{3}{4} \times \frac{5}{9} =$

3. $4 \times \frac{1}{3} =$ $7 \times \frac{3}{4} =$ $6 \times \frac{3}{10} =$ $2 \times \frac{4}{5} =$

4. $\frac{2}{3} \times 1\frac{4}{5} =$ $2\frac{2}{3} \times \frac{1}{5} =$ $3\frac{1}{3} \times \frac{1}{4} =$ $\frac{5}{6} \times 1\frac{3}{4} =$

5. $3 \times 2\frac{1}{3} =$ $5 \times 1\frac{1}{2} =$ $6 \times 1\frac{2}{3} =$ $2 \times \frac{5}{6} =$

6. $2\frac{1}{3} \times 1\frac{3}{4} =$ $1\frac{1}{2} \times 2\frac{2}{3} =$ $4\frac{2}{3} \times 1\frac{4}{5} =$ $2\frac{3}{5} \times 2\frac{5}{6} =$

Math Connection—Grade 5—RBP0172   www.summerbridgeactivities.com   ©RBP Books

Multiplying Fractions

Use the grids to multiply fractions.

$\frac{1}{2} \times \frac{1}{4}$ can be visualized as:

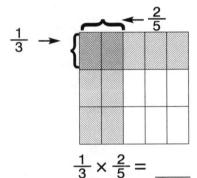

$$\frac{1}{2} \times \frac{1}{4} = \frac{1}{8}$$

$\frac{2}{3} \times \frac{4}{5}$ can be visualized as:

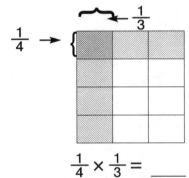

$$\frac{2}{3} \times \frac{4}{5} = \frac{8}{15}$$

1.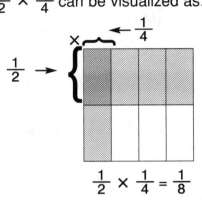

$$\frac{1}{3} \times \frac{2}{5} = \underline{\qquad}$$

2.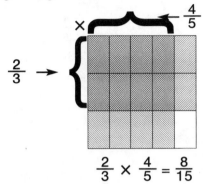

$$\frac{1}{4} \times \frac{1}{3} = \underline{\qquad}$$

3.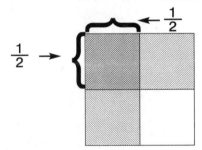

$$\frac{1}{2} \times \frac{1}{2} = \underline{\qquad}$$

4.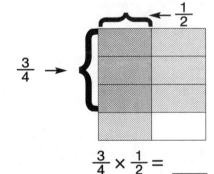

$$\frac{3}{4} \times \frac{1}{2} = \underline{\qquad}$$

5.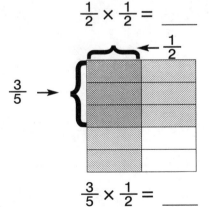

$$\frac{3}{5} \times \frac{1}{2} = \underline{\qquad}$$

6.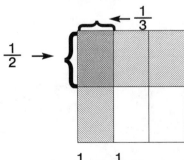

$$\frac{1}{2} \times \frac{1}{3} = \underline{\qquad}$$

© RBP Books   www.summerbridgeactivities.com   Math Connection—Grade 5—RBP0172

Multiplying Fractions

Multiply.

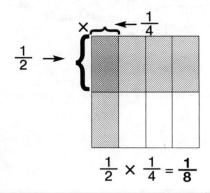

When multiplying $\frac{1}{2} \times \frac{1}{4}$:

$\frac{1}{2} \times \frac{1}{4} = \frac{1}{8}$

Multiply the numerators.
Multiply the denominators.

$$\frac{1}{2} \times \frac{1}{4} = \frac{1 \times 1}{2 \times 4} = \frac{1}{8}$$

$$\frac{3}{4} \times \frac{1}{7} = \frac{1 \times 3}{4 \times 7} = \frac{3}{28}$$

1. $\frac{1}{2} \times \frac{3}{4} =$ $\frac{2}{3} \times \frac{1}{5} =$ $\frac{2}{5} \times \frac{1}{3} =$ $\frac{5}{6} \times \frac{1}{2} =$

2. $\frac{1}{4} \times \frac{3}{8} =$ $\frac{5}{12} \times \frac{1}{2} =$ $\frac{1}{2} \times \frac{5}{7} =$ $\frac{1}{3} \times \frac{1}{4} =$

3. $\frac{1}{5} \times \frac{2}{5} =$ $\frac{3}{5} \times \frac{1}{2} =$ $\frac{3}{4} \times \frac{3}{5} =$ $\frac{3}{4} \times \frac{1}{8} =$

4. $\frac{2}{5} \times \frac{3}{5} =$ $\frac{1}{2} \times \frac{1}{2} =$ $\frac{2}{3} \times \frac{2}{3} =$ $\frac{3}{8} \times \frac{1}{2} =$

5. $\frac{5}{7} \times \frac{1}{3} =$ $\frac{1}{2} \times \frac{3}{7} =$ $\frac{5}{8} \times \frac{1}{3} =$ $\frac{5}{6} \times \frac{1}{3} =$

6. $\frac{3}{5} \times \frac{1}{7} =$ $\frac{1}{8} \times \frac{1}{2} =$ $\frac{1}{4} \times \frac{3}{7} =$ $\frac{5}{9} \times \frac{1}{2} =$

Math Connection—Grade 5—RBP0172   www.summerbridgeactivities.com   ©RBP Books

Multiplying Fractions

Multiply. Simplify if possible.

$\frac{1}{3} \times \frac{3}{8} = \frac{1 \times 3}{3 \times 8}$

$= \frac{3}{24}$

$= \frac{1}{8}$

When multiplying fractions:
1. Multiply the numerators.
2. Multiply the denominators.
3. Simplify if possible.

$\frac{3}{4} \times \frac{4}{5} = \frac{3 \times 4}{4 \times 5}$

$= \frac{12}{20}$

$= \frac{3}{5}$

1. $\frac{3}{8} \times \frac{2}{3} =$ $\qquad$ $\frac{4}{5} \times \frac{1}{2} =$ $\qquad$ $\frac{1}{3} \times \frac{6}{7} =$ $\qquad$ $\frac{1}{2} \times \frac{4}{7} =$

2. $\frac{2}{3} \times \frac{5}{6} =$ $\qquad$ $\frac{1}{3} \times \frac{3}{10} =$ $\qquad$ $\frac{4}{9} \times \frac{3}{4} =$ $\qquad$ $\frac{5}{6} \times \frac{3}{10} =$

3. $\frac{3}{8} \times \frac{1}{6} =$ $\qquad$ $\frac{2}{3} \times \frac{6}{7} =$ $\qquad$ $\frac{5}{6} \times \frac{1}{10} =$ $\qquad$ $\frac{3}{8} \times \frac{4}{9} =$

4. $\frac{3}{10} \times \frac{5}{8} =$ $\qquad$ $\frac{3}{5} \times \frac{2}{9} =$ $\qquad$ $\frac{3}{7} \times \frac{2}{3} =$ $\qquad$ $\frac{2}{3} \times \frac{1}{4} =$

5. $\frac{1}{2} \times \frac{2}{7} =$ $\qquad$ $\frac{5}{8} \times \frac{2}{5} =$ $\qquad$ $\frac{5}{6} \times \frac{2}{5} =$ $\qquad$ $\frac{2}{5} \times \frac{1}{2} =$

©RBP Books www.summerbridgeactivities.com Math Connection—Grade 5—RBP0172

Multiplying Fractions

Multiply. Simplify if possible.

1. $\frac{3}{8} \times \frac{1}{6} =$ $\frac{4}{5} \times \frac{1}{4} =$ $\frac{1}{2} \times \frac{6}{7} =$ $\frac{1}{4} \times \frac{4}{7} =$

2. $\frac{1}{3} \times \frac{6}{11} =$ $\frac{5}{12} \times \frac{3}{4} =$ $\frac{2}{9} \times \frac{3}{4} =$ $\frac{5}{9} \times \frac{3}{5} =$

3. $\frac{4}{9} \times \frac{1}{6} =$ $\frac{1}{6} \times \frac{6}{7} =$ $\frac{5}{12} \times \frac{3}{5} =$ $\frac{5}{6} \times \frac{4}{9} =$

4. $\frac{2}{3} \times \frac{6}{7} =$ $\frac{1}{4} \times \frac{2}{5} =$ $\frac{3}{4} \times \frac{4}{5} =$ $\frac{1}{3} \times \frac{3}{5} =$

5. $\frac{5}{9} \times \frac{3}{10} =$ $\frac{6}{7} \times \frac{7}{9} =$ $\frac{5}{8} \times \frac{2}{5} =$ $\frac{7}{8} \times \frac{5}{7} =$

6. $\frac{8}{15} \times \frac{5}{8} =$ $\frac{11}{12} \times \frac{6}{7} =$ $\frac{3}{10} \times \frac{5}{7} =$ $\frac{5}{12} \times \frac{3}{10} =$

Math Connection—Grade 5—RBP0172

www.summerbridgeactivities.com   ©RBP Books

Multiplying Fractions by Whole Numbers

Multiply. Simplify if possible.

When multiplying a whole number and a fraction:

$$8 \times \frac{3}{8} = \frac{8}{1} \times \frac{3}{8}$$
$$= \frac{8 \times 3}{1 \times 8}$$
$$= \frac{24}{8}$$
$$= 3$$

1. Rewrite the whole number as a fraction (write a denominator of 1).
2. Multiply the numerators.
3. Multiply the denominators.
4. Simplify if possible.

$$\frac{3}{4} \times 6 = \frac{3}{4} \times \frac{6}{1}$$
$$= \frac{3 \times 6}{4 \times 1}$$
$$= \frac{18}{4}$$
$$= 4\frac{2}{4} = 4\frac{1}{2}$$

1. $3 \times \frac{2}{3} =$ $\frac{4}{5} \times 2 =$ $1 \times \frac{6}{7} =$ $2 \times \frac{4}{7} =$

2. $\frac{2}{5} \times 6 =$ $3 \times \frac{3}{10} =$ $9 \times \frac{3}{4} =$ $6 \times \frac{3}{10} =$

3. $8 \times \frac{1}{6} =$ $2 \times \frac{6}{7} =$ $6 \times \frac{1}{10} =$ $\frac{3}{8} \times 4 =$

4. $\frac{3}{10} \times 5 =$ $5 \times \frac{2}{9} =$ $\frac{3}{7} \times 2 =$ $\frac{2}{3} \times 4 =$

© RBP Books   www.summerbridgeactivities.com   Math Connection—Grade 5—RBP0172

Name _____   Date _____

Multiplying Mixed Numbers by Fractions
Multiply. Simplify if possible.

When multiplying a mixed number and a fraction:

$$2\frac{1}{3} \times \frac{4}{5} = \frac{7}{3} \times \frac{4}{5}$$
$$= \frac{7 \times 4}{3 \times 5}$$
$$= \frac{28}{15}$$
$$= 1\frac{13}{15}$$

1. Rewrite the mixed number as an improper fraction.
2. Multiply the numerators.
3. Multiply the denominators.
4. Simplify if possible.

$$\frac{1}{3} \times 2\frac{2}{3} = \frac{1}{3} \times \frac{8}{3}$$
$$= \frac{1 \times 8}{3 \times 3}$$
$$= \frac{8}{9}$$

1. $\frac{1}{2} \times 1\frac{1}{8} =$ $2\frac{1}{3} \times \frac{1}{3} =$ $4\frac{1}{2} \times \frac{1}{3} =$ $2\frac{2}{3} \times \frac{3}{7} =$

2. $3\frac{1}{2} \times \frac{1}{4} =$ $\frac{3}{5} \times 3\frac{1}{2} =$ $\frac{2}{5} \times 3\frac{1}{3} =$ $\frac{2}{3} \times 5\frac{1}{4} =$

3. $4\frac{3}{4} \times \frac{1}{3} =$ $\frac{1}{9} \times 2\frac{1}{2} =$ $\frac{1}{2} \times 1\frac{3}{5} =$ $\frac{1}{6} \times 3\frac{1}{3} =$

4. $4\frac{2}{3} \times \frac{3}{4} =$ $9\frac{1}{2} \times \frac{1}{6} =$ $3\frac{3}{4} \times \frac{5}{12} =$ $2\frac{1}{3} \times \frac{3}{8} =$

Math Connection—Grade 5—RBP0172   www.summerbridgeactivities.com   ©RBP Books

Multiplying Mixed Numbers by Whole Numbers

Multiply. Simplify if possible.

When multiplying a mixed and a whole number:

$2\frac{1}{3} \times 4 = \frac{7}{3} \times \frac{4}{1}$

$\phantom{2\frac{1}{3} \times 4 } = \frac{7 \times 4}{3 \times 1}$

$\phantom{2\frac{1}{3} \times 4 } = \frac{28}{3}$

$\phantom{2\frac{1}{3} \times 4 } = 9\frac{1}{3}$

1. Rewrite the numbers as improper fractions.
2. Multiply the numerators.
3. Multiply the denominators.
4. Simplify if possible.

$6 \times 3\frac{2}{3} = \frac{6}{1} \times \frac{11}{3}$

$\phantom{6 \times 3\frac{2}{3} } = \frac{6 \times 11}{1 \times 3}$

$\phantom{6 \times 3\frac{2}{3} } = \frac{66}{3}$

$\phantom{6 \times 3\frac{2}{3} } = 22$

1. $3\frac{1}{4} \times 2 =$ $1\frac{4}{5} \times 2 =$ $1 \times 3\frac{6}{7} =$ $2 \times 4\frac{4}{7} =$

2. $3\frac{2}{5} \times 2 =$ $3 \times 2\frac{3}{10} =$ $9 \times 1\frac{3}{4} =$ $3 \times 4\frac{3}{10} =$

3. $3 \times 4\frac{1}{6} =$ $2 \times 3\frac{6}{7} =$ $6 \times 2\frac{1}{10} =$ $5\frac{3}{8} \times 4 =$

4. $2\frac{3}{10} \times 4 =$ $5 \times 2\frac{5}{9} =$ $5\frac{1}{7} \times 2 =$ $6\frac{2}{3} \times 4 =$

Multiplying Mixed Numbers

Multiply. Simplify if possible.

When multiplying mixed numbers:

$2\frac{1}{4} \times 1\frac{1}{2} = \frac{9}{4} \times \frac{3}{2}$

$\qquad = \frac{9 \times 3}{4 \times 2}$

$\qquad = \frac{27}{8}$

$\qquad = 3\frac{3}{8}$

1. Rewrite the numbers as improper fractions.
2. Multiply the numerators.
3. Multiply the denominators.
4. Simplify if possible.

$1\frac{1}{3} \times 2\frac{1}{8} = \frac{4}{3} \times \frac{17}{8}$

$\qquad = \frac{4 \times 17}{3 \times 8}$

$\qquad = \frac{68}{24}$

$\qquad = 2\frac{20}{24} = \mathbf{2\frac{5}{6}}$

1. $3\frac{3}{4} \times 2\frac{2}{3} =$ $\qquad$ $1\frac{1}{4} \times 2\frac{1}{2} =$ $\qquad$ $2\frac{1}{5} \times 2\frac{1}{4} =$ $\qquad$ $1\frac{1}{5} \times 2\frac{1}{6} =$

2. $1\frac{3}{5} \times 1\frac{2}{5} =$ $\qquad$ $2\frac{1}{2} \times 3\frac{1}{3} =$ $\qquad$ $4\frac{1}{2} \times 1\frac{2}{3} =$ $\qquad$ $2\frac{4}{5} \times 5\frac{1}{4} =$

3. $2\frac{3}{8} \times 2\frac{1}{3} =$ $\qquad$ $1\frac{4}{5} \times 1\frac{1}{4} =$ $\qquad$ $1\frac{3}{7} \times 1\frac{3}{8} =$ $\qquad$ $1\frac{1}{2} \times 3\frac{2}{3} =$

4. $4\frac{1}{2} \times 1\frac{2}{5} =$ $\qquad$ $3\frac{2}{3} \times 1\frac{1}{2} =$ $\qquad$ $4\frac{1}{2} \times 1\frac{1}{2} =$ $\qquad$ $2\frac{3}{8} \times 3\frac{2}{7} =$

Math Connection—Grade 5—RBP0172   www.summerbridgeactivities.com   ©RBP Books

Multiplying Fractions

Multiply. Simplify if possible.

1. $\dfrac{3}{4} \times \dfrac{1}{2} =$ $\dfrac{1}{3} \times \dfrac{2}{5} =$ $\dfrac{4}{5} \times \dfrac{1}{3} =$ $\dfrac{5}{8} \times \dfrac{3}{4} =$

2. $\dfrac{2}{3} \times \dfrac{3}{5} =$ $\dfrac{4}{5} \times \dfrac{5}{9} =$ $\dfrac{3}{8} \times \dfrac{4}{5} =$ $\dfrac{1}{5} \times \dfrac{10}{11} =$

3. $6 \times \dfrac{1}{3} =$ $5 \times \dfrac{1}{2} =$ $\dfrac{2}{3} \times 8 =$ $\dfrac{4}{5} \times 7 =$

4. $\dfrac{2}{3} \times 1\dfrac{1}{2} =$ $1\dfrac{4}{5} \times \dfrac{1}{3} =$ $2\dfrac{1}{4} \times \dfrac{1}{3} =$ $3\dfrac{3}{4} \times \dfrac{1}{2} =$

5. $2\dfrac{3}{4} \times 5 =$ $2 \times 1\dfrac{1}{2} =$ $5 \times 2\dfrac{1}{5} =$ $1\dfrac{1}{3} \times 4 =$

6. $1\dfrac{3}{4} \times 2\dfrac{1}{3} =$ $1\dfrac{1}{2} \times 2\dfrac{1}{2} =$ $2\dfrac{1}{4} \times 1\dfrac{1}{4} =$ $1\dfrac{2}{5} \times 2\dfrac{1}{6} =$

Whoa! I'm multiplying!

© RBP Books   www.summerbridgeactivities.com   Math Connection—Grade 5—RBP0172

Problem Solving

1. Austin is going to the movie theater. It is $3\frac{3}{5}$ miles from his house. Austin decides to take his electric scooter, but it breaks down $\frac{2}{3}$ of the way there. How far is Austin from his house?

2. Austin's electric scooter uses $\frac{1}{4}$ gallon of fuel each mile. How much fuel has he used? (Hint: Use your answer from question 1.)

3. Austin purchases $\frac{2}{3}$ pound of yum-yum treats. If yum-yum treats are $6.00 per pound, how much does Austin pay?

4. In the theater, Austin meets his 2 friends, who have purchased 1 gigantic barrel of popcorn. Only $\frac{3}{4}$ of it is left. Austin eats $\frac{1}{3}$ of what was left. How much of the barrel did Austin eat?

5. After the movie, Austin starts walking home. He walks $\frac{1}{6}$ of the $3\frac{3}{5}$ miles to his house before his mom picks him up. How far did Austin walk?

© RBP Books www.summerbridgeactivities.com **Math Connection—Grade 5—RBP0172**

Problem Solving

1. Jacob's class has 24 students. If $\frac{1}{8}$ of them play the piano, how many students in his class play the piano?

2. There are 12 students working in the library. If $\frac{3}{4}$ of them are girls, how many girls are in the library?

3. Six students are working on math. Two-thirds of them are working on fractions. How many students are working on fractions?

4. Jacob spent half of his $1\frac{1}{2}$-hour gym class jumping rope. How long did he spend jumping rope?

5. Jacob's class spent $1\frac{3}{4}$ hours in science class. Two-thirds of the time was spent studying insects. How much time did he spend studying insects?

Post-Test: Multiplying Fractions

1. $\frac{2}{5} \times \frac{1}{3} =$ $\frac{1}{4} \times \frac{5}{6} =$ $\frac{5}{6} \times \frac{1}{3} =$ $\frac{7}{10} \times \frac{1}{3} =$

2. $\frac{1}{3} \times \frac{6}{11} =$ $\frac{1}{2} \times \frac{6}{7} =$ $\frac{3}{7} \times \frac{1}{6} =$ $\frac{9}{10} \times \frac{5}{12} =$

3. $2 \times \frac{2}{3} =$ $8 \times \frac{3}{4} =$ $4 \times \frac{5}{12} =$ $5 \times \frac{2}{5} =$

4. $\frac{2}{3} \times 2\frac{4}{7} =$ $1\frac{2}{5} \times \frac{5}{8} =$ $3\frac{1}{8} \times \frac{2}{3} =$ $\frac{5}{6} \times 2\frac{1}{4} =$

5. $1 \times 3\frac{2}{3} =$ $5 \times 1\frac{1}{4} =$ $6 \times 2\frac{3}{4} =$ $2 \times 3\frac{4}{9} =$

6. $2\frac{1}{3} \times 2\frac{3}{4} =$ $1\frac{1}{5} \times 1\frac{2}{3} =$ $3\frac{2}{5} \times 1\frac{2}{3} =$ $2\frac{1}{2} \times 1\frac{5}{12} =$

© RBP Books   www.summerbridgeactivities.com   Math Connection—Grade 5—RBP0172

Number Patterns

1. $\frac{1}{2}$, 1, $\frac{3}{2}$, 2, $\frac{5}{2}$, 3, ____, ____, ____

2. $\frac{1}{4}$, $\frac{1}{2}$, $\frac{3}{4}$, 1, $\frac{5}{4}$, $\frac{3}{2}$, ____, ____, ____

3. $\frac{1}{2}$, $\frac{1}{4}$, $\frac{1}{8}$, $\frac{1}{16}$, ____, ____, ____

4. $\frac{1}{3}$, 1, $1\frac{2}{3}$, $2\frac{1}{3}$, 3, $3\frac{2}{3}$, ____, ____, ____

5. $\frac{1}{5}$, $\frac{3}{5}$, $\frac{9}{5}$, $\frac{27}{5}$, ____, ____, ____

6. $\frac{1}{7}$, $\frac{1}{6}$, $\frac{1}{5}$, $\frac{1}{4}$, ____, ____, ____

7. $\frac{4}{3}$, $\frac{7}{6}$, 1, $\frac{5}{6}$, $\frac{2}{3}$, ____, ____, ____

8. 8, $7\frac{1}{2}$, 7, $6\frac{1}{2}$, ____, ____, ____

9. $5\frac{1}{3}$, 5, $4\frac{2}{3}$, $4\frac{1}{3}$, ____, ____, ____

10. $\frac{2}{5}$, $\frac{3}{10}$, $\frac{4}{15}$, $\frac{5}{20}$, ____, ____, ____

Math Connection—Grade 5—RBP0172   www.summerbridgeactivities.com   © RBP Books

Decimals

You should already know the place value names for numbers bigger than 0. There are also names for place values after the decimal place.

thousands	hundreds	tens	ones		tenths	hundredths	thousandths
1	2	4	5	.	1	7	6

Study the following:

DECIMAL	READ AS	EQUIVALENT FRACTION
.1	one-tenth	$\frac{1}{10}$
.7	seven-tenths	$\frac{7}{10}$
.23	twenty-three hundredths	$\frac{23}{100}$
.05	five-hundredths	$\frac{5}{100}$
.783	seven hundred eighty-three thousandths	$\frac{783}{1000}$
.045	forty-five thousandths	$\frac{45}{1000}$
2.6	two and six-tenths	$2\frac{6}{10}$
15.01	fifteen and one-hundredth	$15\frac{1}{100}$

Hint: "and" separates the whole number from the fraction.

Complete.

1.	.3	three-tenths	_____
2.	1.12	_____	_____
3.	_____	two hundred twenty-one thousandths	_____
4.	_____	_____	$\frac{53}{100}$
5.	.871	_____	_____
6.	_____	_____	$2\frac{1}{100}$

Name _____ Date _____

Equivalent Decimals and Fractions

Study how to rewrite decimals and fractions.

$\frac{4}{10} = .4$

$5\frac{874}{1000} = 5.874$

$5.78 = 5\frac{78}{100}$

$1.521 = 1\frac{521}{1000}$

Write the following fractions as decimals.

1. $4\frac{4}{10}$ _____ $\frac{23}{100}$ _____

2. $1\frac{3}{100}$ _____ $\frac{5}{10}$ _____

3. $\frac{548}{1000}$ _____ $2\frac{53}{100}$ _____

4. $53\frac{17}{100}$ _____ $16\frac{303}{1000}$ _____

5. $\frac{91}{1000}$ _____ $91\frac{3}{10}$ _____

Write the following decimals as mixed fractions.

6. 2.87 _____   .983 _____

7. 14.5 _____   287.69 _____

8. 1.752 _____   .7 _____

9. .06 _____   10.054 _____

10. 81.2 _____   .157 _____

© RBP Books   www.summerbridgeactivities.com   Math Connection—Grade 5—RBP0172

Visualizing Decimals

Complete the following.

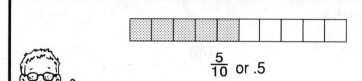

$\frac{5}{10}$ or .5

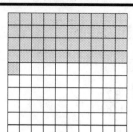

$\frac{41}{100}$ or .41

	Fraction	Decimal
1.	_____	_____
2.	_____	_____
3.	_____	_____
4.	_____	_____
5.	_____	_____
6.	_____	_____
7.	_____	_____

Name _____ Date _____

Comparing Decimals

Put the correct sign (>, <, =) in each problem.

> Comparing decimals is similar to comparing whole numbers.
> 1. Line up the numbers by place value.
> 2. Compare the digits left to right.
>
> **Example 1** .08 ◯ .8
>
> 1. Line up: .08
>   .8
>
> 2. Compare.
> After the decimal point, you have a 0 and an 8. 8 is bigger than 0, so .8 is bigger.
>   .08 (<) .8
>
> **Example 2** 11.13 ◯ 11.03
>
>   11.13
>   11.03
>
> The 11's before the decimal point are the same. After the decimal point, is 1 or 0 bigger? 1 is.
>   11.13 (>) 11.03

1. .007 ◯ .07

2. 2.159 ◯ 2.259

3. 10.05 ◯ 10.005

4. 0.99 ◯ .009

5. 30.249 ◯ 30.429

6. .004 ◯ 4.00

7. 6.041 ◯ 6.401

8. 92.001 ◯ 92.001

9. 263.08 ◯ 263.81

10. .08 ◯ .8

11. 101.05 ◯ 101.005

12. 9.50 ◯ 7.05

13. 214.01 ◯ 214.001

14. 9.008 ◯ 9.08

15. 614.05 ◯ 614.05

16. 8.26 ◯ 8.026

17. 43.014 ◯ 43.104

18. .83 ◯ .63

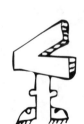

© RBP Books   www.summerbridgeactivities.com   Math Connection—Grade 5—RBP0172

Menu Mix-up

Put the prices on the menu in order from least to greatest.

$1.25 $2.03 $1.07 $2.51 $1.10 $2.15 $2.21 $1.05

Item:	Price:
Soda	
Milk	
Fries	
Salad	
Cheese Sandwich	
Tuna Sandwich	
Hamburger	
Cheeseburger	

Circle the largest decimal number in each row.

1. 4.05   4.50   4.005   4.15   4.55   4.5

2. 10.57   10.49   10.005   10.057   10.75   10.094

3. 2.5   2.15   2.52   2.005   2.095   2.51

4. 1.8   1.84   1.48   1.847   1.75   1.5

5. 89.90   88.19   8.90   89.09   89.5   89.01

Geometry: Lines

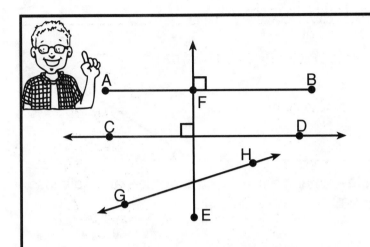

$\overline{AB}$ is a **line segment**.

$\overleftrightarrow{CD}$ and $\overleftrightarrow{GH}$ are **lines**.

$\overrightarrow{EF}$ is a **ray**.

$\overline{AB}$ is **parallel** to $\overleftrightarrow{CD}$.

$\overleftrightarrow{GH}$ and $\overleftrightarrow{CD}$ are **intersecting** lines.

$\overrightarrow{EF}$ is **perpendicular** to $\overline{AB}$ and $\overleftrightarrow{CD}$.

$\overleftrightarrow{GH}$ and $\overrightarrow{EF}$ **intersect**.

Classify each. Circle the best answer.

1.    line   line segment   ray

2.   line   line segment   ray

3.   line   line segment   ray

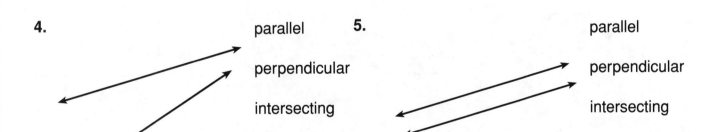

4.   parallel   perpendicular   intersecting   **5.**   parallel   perpendicular   intersecting

6.   parallel   perpendicular   intersecting   **7.**   parallel   perpendicular   intersecting

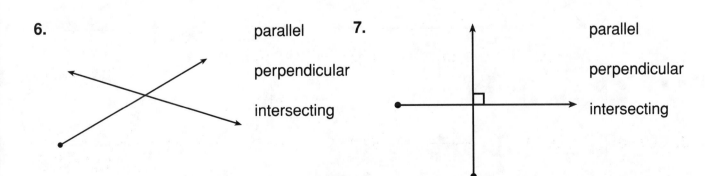

Geometry: Angles

Write the name for each type of angle.

 An angle is two lines with a common end point.

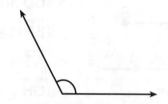

90˚

Right angle—formed when two lines are perpendicular (90˚)

Obtuse angle—an angle greater than 90˚

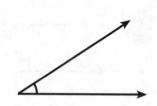

Acute angle—an angle less than 90˚

1. 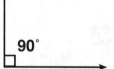 _____

  _____

2. 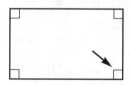 _____

  _____

3.   _____

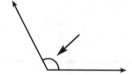 _____

4. 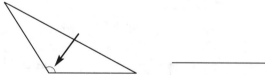 _____

  _____

5.   _____

  _____

Math Connection—Grade 5—RBP0172   www.summerbridgeactivities.com   © RBP Books

Name ______________________________ Date ______________________________

Geometry: Polygons

Write the general name for each of the following figures.

Some polygons have more than one classification. These are the general names of polygons, named for the number of sides.

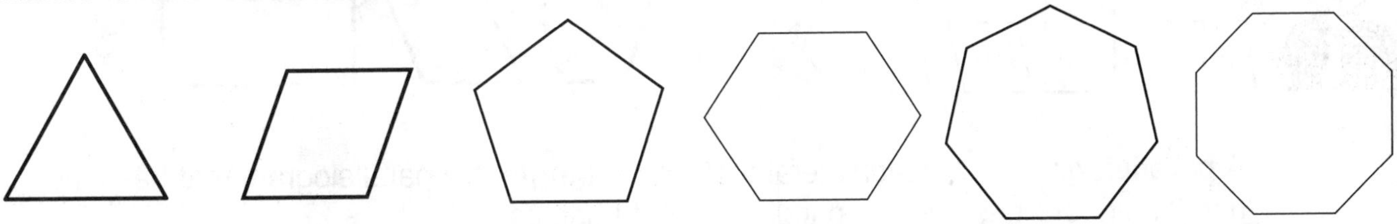

triangle = 3 sides	quadrilateral = _____ sides	pentagon = 5 sides	hexagon = _____ sides	heptagon = 7 sides	octagon = _____ sides

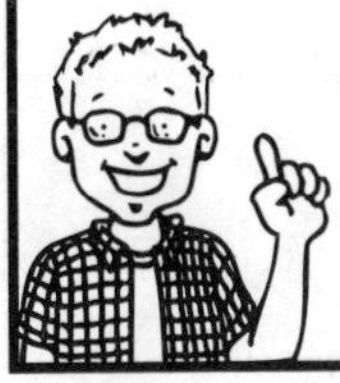

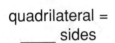

A square is a quadrilateral because it has 4 sides.

1.

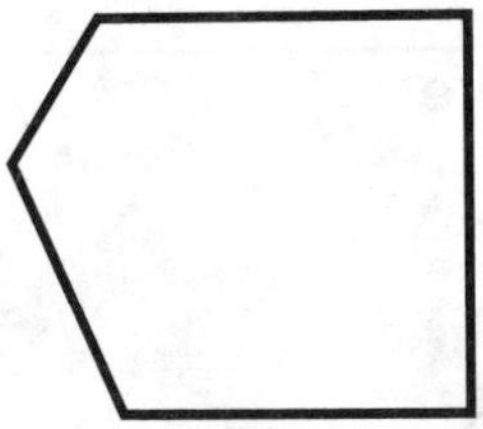

____

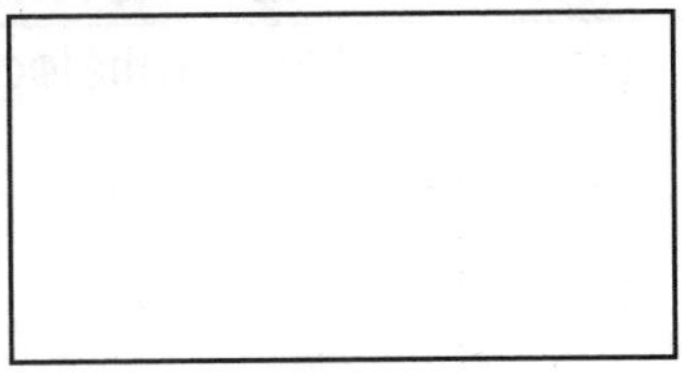

____

2.

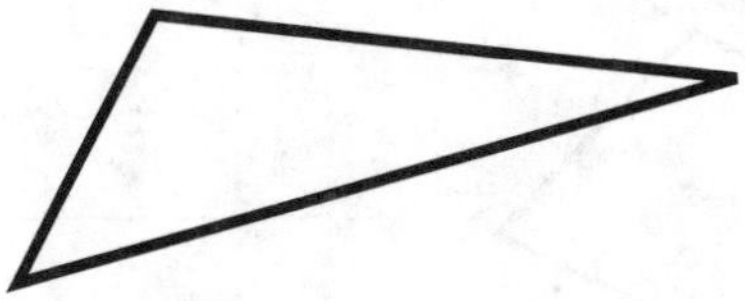

____

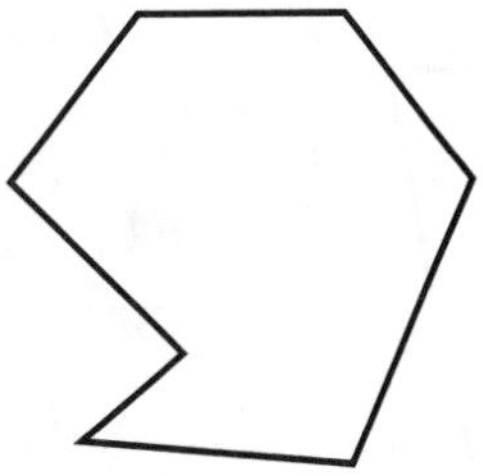

____

3.

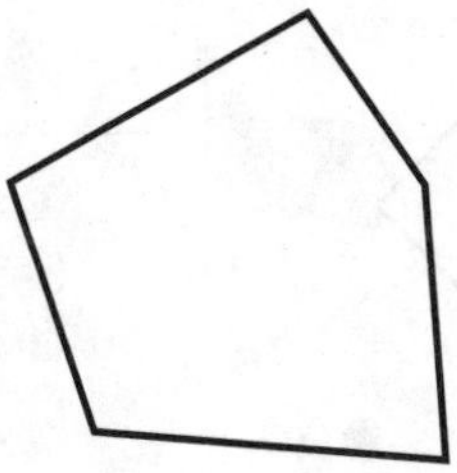

____

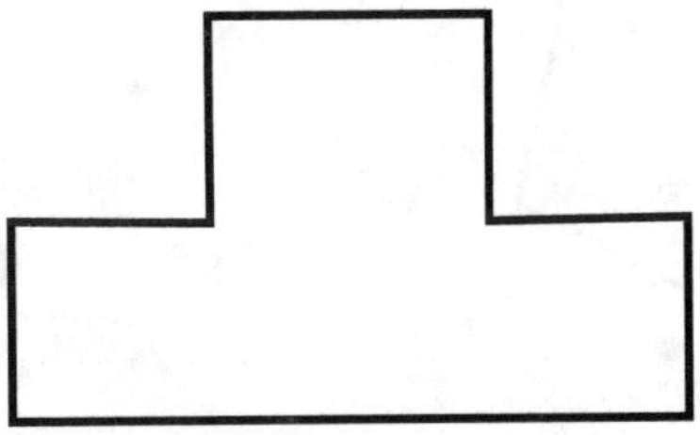

____

©RBP Books

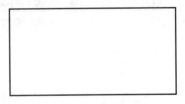

Geometry: Quadrilaterals

A **quadrilateral** has 4 sides.

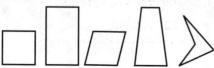

A **trapezoid** has at least 1 pair of parallel sides.

A **parallelogram** is a quadrilateral that has 2 pairs of sides that are parallel.

A **rectangle** is a parallelogram that has four right angles.

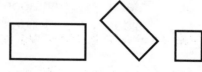

A **square** is a rectangle that has four equal lengths.

Classify the following quadrilaterals.

(**a**) quadrilateral (**b**) trapezoid (**c**) parallelogram (**d**) rectangle (**e**) square

1. 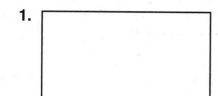 _____   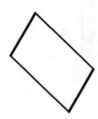 _____

2. 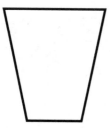 _____   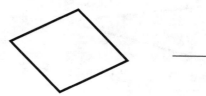 _____

3. 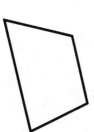 _____   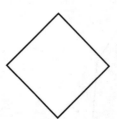 _____

Math Connection—Grade 5—RBP0172   www.summerbridgeactivities.com   © RBP Books

Geometry: Congruent and Similar

> **Congruent** polygons have equal lengths and angles.
> **Similar** polygons have equal angles.

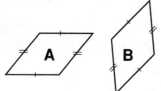   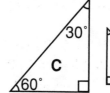

Parallelograms A and B are **congruent**.   Triangles C and D are **similar** triangles.

Classify each pair as similar or congruent.

1.

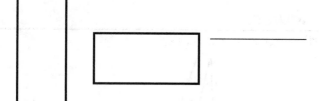

2.

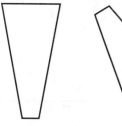    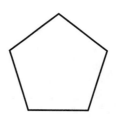

3.

 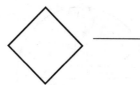   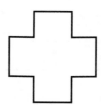 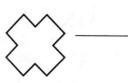

© RBP Books   www.summerbridgeactivities.com   Math Connection—Grade 5—RBP0172

Name _____ Date _____

Geometry: Three-Dimensional Objects

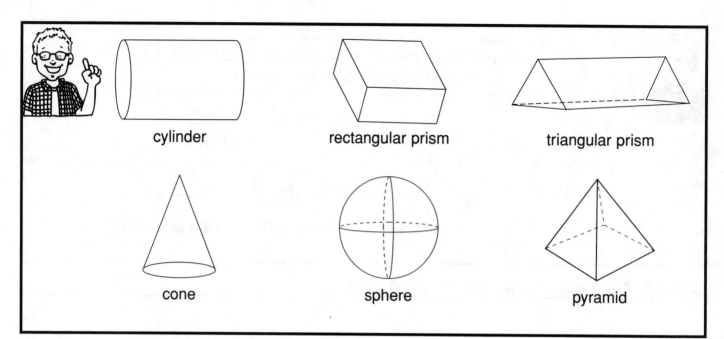

cylinder   rectangular prism   triangular prism

cone   sphere   pyramid

Write the name for each of the following figures.

1.
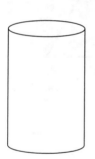 _____    _____

2.
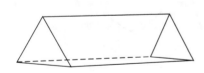 _____    _____

3.
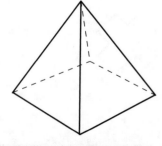 _____   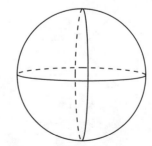 _____

Math Connection—Grade 5—RBP0172   144   www.summerbridgeactivities.com   ©RBP Books

Geometry: Three-Dimensional Objects

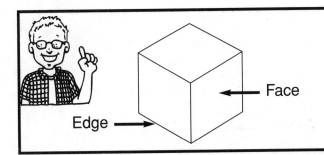

Face

Edge

A cube has 6 **faces** (sides). A **face** is a flat surface.

A cube has 12 **edges**. An **edge** is a segment where two faces meet.

Name the number of faces and edges for each figure.

faces   edges

1.

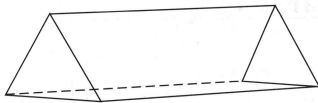

_____   _____

2.

_____   _____

3.

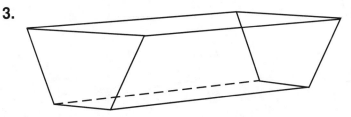

_____   _____

4.

_____   _____

5.

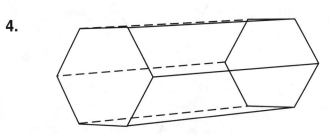

_____   _____

© RBP Books   www.summerbridgeactivities.com   Math Connection—Grade 5—RBP0172

Geometry: Problem Solving

If a figure can be folded along a line so that the 2 halves match perfectly, then the line is a **line of symmetry**. A square has 4 lines of symmetry.

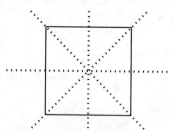

Draw the lines of symmetry for each object. Write the number of lines of symmetry.

1.
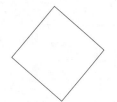 Lines: _____
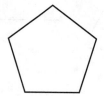 Lines: _____
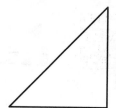 Lines: _____

2.
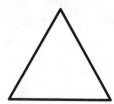 Lines: _____
  Lines: _____
  Lines: _____

3.
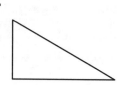 Lines: _____
 Lines: _____
 Lines: _____

4.
 Lines: _____
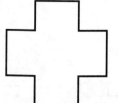 Lines: _____
 Lines: _____

Math Connection—Grade 5—RBP0172   www.summerbridgeactivities.com   ©RBP Books

Geometry: Problem Solving

Draw a new figure by following the directions given.

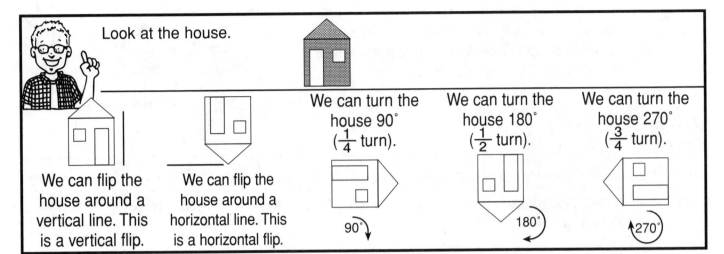

Look at the house.

We can flip the house around a vertical line. This is a vertical flip.

We can flip the house around a horizontal line. This is a horizontal flip.

We can turn the house 90° ($\frac{1}{4}$ turn).

We can turn the house 180° ($\frac{1}{2}$ turn).

We can turn the house 270° ($\frac{3}{4}$ turn).

1. Flip horizontally.

2. Turn 90° ($\frac{1}{4}$ turn).

3. Turn 180° ($\frac{1}{2}$ turn).

4. Flip vertically.

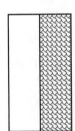

5. Turn 270° ($\frac{3}{4}$ turn).

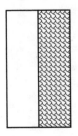

6. Flip vertically and turn 90°.

© RBP Books www.summerbridgeactivities.com   **Math Connection—Grade 5—RBP0172**

Real-Life Problem Solving: Using What We Know
A radio station is giving tickets away to an upcoming concert by the Frac-tones.

1. The station will give away 525 tickets. The concert arena can hold 1,658 people. How many tickets are left?

2. Jason knows the words to $\frac{2}{3}$ of the Frac-tones songs. If the Frac-tones have 21 songs, how many of their songs does Jason know?

3. The opening act for the Frac-tones will be the Numerators. They will sing 3 songs. The songs will last 7 minutes 13 seconds, 5 minutes 6 seconds, and 4 minutes 20 seconds. How much total time will the Numerators spend singing?

4. The cost per ticket for the public is $15. If the public purchases all the remaining tickets, how much money will the concert make? (Hint: Use your answer from problem 1.)

5. How much are the 525 tickets that the radio station is giving away worth?

Real-Life Problem Solving: Using What We Know

A local basketball team (the Buzzers) recently played a rival team and won 84 to 82.

1. If Joe Johnson scored 14 points (out of the total score of 84), what fraction of the Buzzers' total points did Joe score?

2. The Buzzers made four 3-pointers.
   a. How many points were made by 3-point shots?

   b. What fraction of the points were 3-point shots?

3. The game lasted 140 minutes. If $\frac{3}{7}$ of the time was spent for time outs, how many minutes were spent in time out?

4. One-fourth of the Buzzers' points were made by Carl Malley. How many points did Carl make?

5. A college or high school basketball court is 84 feet long by 50 feet wide. An NBA court is 94 by 50 feet long.
   a. What is the area of each court?

   b. What is the difference between the areas?

© RBP Books   www.summerbridgeactivities.com   Math Connection—Grade 5—RBP0172

Real-Life Problem Solving: Using What We Know

Rebecca is planning a vacation trip for her family of 4 from Denver, Colorado, to San Diego, California.

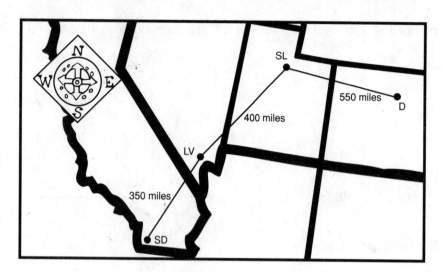

1. If they drive, using the map above, what is the distance from Denver to San Diego?

2. By looking at the map above, how much further is it from Denver to Salt Lake than from Salt Lake to Las Vegas?

3. Rebecca found a round trip flight for $322 per ticket. Or, she can get four tickets together for $1,196. How much would she save by buying the four tickets together?

4. If they drive, Rebecca plans on spending $250 for two hotels (in Salt Lake and Las Vegas). She also figures it will cost $114 in gasoline to drive.
   a. Is it cheaper to drive or fly her family?

   b. How much would she save?

Answer Pages

Page 5
1. 9 17 16 14 8 9 11 13
2. 5 12 14 8 18 11 4 10
3. 13 12 9 16 8 11 2 15
4. 5 6 4 10 15 14 13 16
5. 14 6 3 7 10 11 7 15
6. 12 11 6 10 11 11 13 6
7. 9 14 3 13 9 8 6 16
8. 9 12 10 18 13 10 12 16
9. 12 8 10 8 9 14 10 6
10. 4 15 10 5 11 12 3 10

Page 6
1. 14 8 5 9 11 9 12 13
2. 10 11 13 16 11 12 6 10
3. 14 10 15 7 14 9 17 8
4. 9 9 2 5 7 5 7 13
5. 13 10 7 17 12 6 10 11
6. 13 3 8 14 11 8 12 14
7. 10 11 17 12 10 13 12 7
8. 4 11 9 15 9 7 9 11
9. 9 15 10 12 6 14 12 13
10. 11 11 15 8 10 3 14 13

Page 7
1. 1 5 6 3 2 7 8 1
2. 6 1 4 2 9 9 1 0
3. 3 6 8 5 8 7 8 8
4. 3 8 6 4 12 7 5 3
5. 4 1 9 2 6 8 6 9
6. 9 2 3 2 1 2 5 5
7. 1 1 4 7 9 9 3 6
8. 7 9 9 5 6 0 3 8
9. 0 3 4 8 8 4 5 0
10. 2 3 1 4 4 7 2 7

Page 8
1. 9 7 1 8 3 1 4 4
2. 8 2 3 3 2 1 7 6
3. 9 8 3 8 4 9 9 5
4. 8 2 6 1 4 9 4 8
5. 6 4 9 4 9 3 6 9
6. 2 2 8 8 2 8 1 6
7. 5 7 2 7 3 3 5 7
8. 6 4 5 3 5 5 6 5
9. 3 2 3 6 5 8 7 6
10. 7 5 4 4 1 1 8 2

Page 9
1. 0 8 45 0 56 24 48 10
2. 12 24 40 35 21 20 18 0
3. 8 7 9 40 42 30 0 32
4. 9 0 54 56 18 49 64 0
5. 45 6 28 72 0 8 24 20
6. 0 12 24 4 15 14 40 15
7. 7 27 21 18 25 28 0 6
8. 42 12 35 16 8 27 0 30
9. 4 24 20 16 3 2 72 5
10. 6 63 81 63 32 0 5 36

Page 10
1. 4 9 18 42 45 14 56 36
2. 35 3 7 48 32 24 21 40
3. 6 30 20 8 9 12 8 10
4. 45 0 6 64 18 14 5 8
5. 54 9 0 28 12 72 16 63
6. 0 18 6 27 12 21 36 36
7. 5 2 27 30 8 28 7 24
8. 0 56 81 18 10 16 24 72
9. 32 63 54 12 3 15 25 42
10. 0 48 0 49 4 6 16 1

Page 11
1. 6 5 6 2 2 4 4
2. 2 2 1 8 5 3 9
3. 7 2 9 7 3 0 7
4. 1 8 9 1 4 6 5
5. 8 5 7 8 9 4 1
6. 0 3 7 1 7 8 6
7. 2 6 2 7 9 2 5
8. 9 3 2 6 3 5 9
9. 8 5 4 1 1 4 7
10. 4 8 9 7 8 8 5

Page 12
1. 9 5 5 7 3 8 4
2. 4 1 2 9 2 5 5
3. 7 3 9 2 7 1 0
4. 6 3 9 9 4 1 2
5. 6 5 1 4 4 6 1
6. 5 7 4 7 3 1 7
7. 6 2 7 2 3 8 2
8. 0 3 9 7 5 8 5
9. 8 3 3 9 4 3 7
10. 8 4 2 4 0 6 2

Page 15
1. 84 112 71 79 117
2. 1,077 1,007 996 1,517 705
3. 10,013 17,646 129,387 292,125 1,357,516
4. 141 1,580 1,140 15,534 177,487
5. 453 20,652 24,519 158,382 187,308
6. 12 27 4 414 540
7. 9 402 270 3,861 995
8. 1,942 1,000 4,055 52,004 10,000

© RBP Books   www.summerbridgeactivities.com   Math Connection—Grade 5—RBP0172

Answer Pages

Page 16
1.	7	10	9	15	12	11	6	14
2.	10	5	13	8	11	4	9	8
3.	11	14	18	12	13	8	5	16
4.	15	7	2	8	9	10	10	7
5.	11	8	11	9	12	11	16	13
6.	12	11	9	4	6	5	10	3
7.	14	13	9	15	10	4	6	17
8.	5	16	7	12	9	7	7	8
9.	9	3	8	10	14	8	6	11
10.	10	5	12	3	14	13	12	6

Page 17
1.	31	97	61	53	54	87
2.	83	74	59	56	79	91
3.	72	95	64	47	89	99
4.	86	56	58	99	34	39
5.	88	95	79	89	79	52
6.	84	69	28	59	76	89
7.	77	46	66	66	86	77
8.	88	98	78	93	81	87

Page 18
1.	55	135	105	94	82	103
2.	113	166	50	119	63	65
3.	116	61	66	187	148	146
4.	93	115	66	153	96	124
5.	86	120	149	91	58	88
6.	184	113	114	112	176	178
7.	85	178	86	125	100	95
8.	84	75	119	135	53	141

Page 19
1.	905	894	824	1,170	936
2.	1,298	1,560	1,003	1,458	899
3.	513	873	1,140	1,324	466
4.	678	1,432	776	891	1,031
5.	538	595	1,170	1,639	1,389
6.	1,145	1,738	539	1,381	385
7.	1,029	865	1,117	1,153	1,236
8.	1,446	269	825	535	1,264

Page 20
1.	9,199	12,788	4,714	12,471	5,323
2.	10,347	9,530	14,552	11,585	10,966
3.	12,264	11,319	7,305	8,567	3,782
4.	12,731	5,110	7,536	13,375	8,031
5.	7,411	18,264	10,623	8,037	10,887
6.	89,562	122,121	93,467	164,259	79,387
7.	51,631	157,245	86,384	61,133	110,615
8.	69,136	98,481	96,215	140,201	76,308

Page 21
1.	1,965	2,381	798	789	1,437
2.	15,301	20,660	13,608	22,532	13,031
3.	1,203	23,745	18,407	125,262	127,881
4.	2,365	2,446	19,957	28,793	135,110
5.	2,709	13,787	114,667	850,878	63,083

Page 22
1.	1	6	5	2	2	2	7	2
2.	5	1	4	3	1	1	4	1
3.	1	1	3	5	1	6	3	8
4.	5	4	4	3	6	7	2	4
5.	3	2	4	2	8	9	7	8
6.	7	9	8	8	9	5	9	6
7.	7	6	3	9	3	0	6	3
8.	9	8	0	8	0	5	7	0

Page 23
1.	66	14	42	24
2.	41	13	40	61
3.	30	24	29	40
4.	2	10	30	24
5.	22	24	51	32
6.	72	31	21	35
7.	34	54	13	15

Page 24
1.	1	68	27	37
2.	11	25	29	49
3.	5	6	73	26
4.	45	19	46	8
5.	47	2	52	44
6.	36	9	8	9
7.	43	27	9	42

Page 25
1.	474	252	671	499	18	1
2.	698	85	502	414	129	551
3.	246	589	73	14	1	23
4.	385	130	790	279	382	125
5.	122	1	368	15	54	186
6.	748	74	232	347	224	87
7.	153	497	236	310	511	249

Page 26
1.	1,063	6,684	1,612	538	791
2.	5,325	2,107	3,449	4,841	3,997
3.	80,967	78,112	80,946	92,290	60,048
4.	51,236	61,911	70,136	31,726	92,591
5.	4,399	58,527	32,813	1,921	44,633
6.	45,434	21,434	5,611	4,462	1,264

Page 27
1. 2,233 seats   **2.** 263 people   **3.** 6,747 people
4. 1,747 people   **5.** 1,593 people

Page 28
1. 1,074   **2.** 2,279   **3.** 279
4. 1,925   **5.** 2,718   **6.** no

Math Connection—Grade 5—RBP0172

www.summerbridgeactivities.com   ©RBP Books

Answer Pages

Page 29

1.	83	131	93	102	101
2.	735	1,020	770	1,031	1,483
3.	5,178	8,274	63,815	148,299	450,045
4.	135	1,962	1,176	14,158	199,584
5.	165	1,560	20,101	111,705	157,808
6.	6	22	16	155	174
7.	46	417	5,405	2,145	2,898
8.	55,109	84,418	39,419	21,112	512,029

Page 30

1. $45   2. $43   3. a. $142 b. $42
4. $16   5. socks & a shirt 6. $35

Page 31

1.	21	30	135	576
2.	2,075	5,154	1,425	1,482
3.	19,874	39,273	54,240	14,469
4.	143,982	525,866	561,476	211,820
5.	2,827,576	4,117,496	5,907,122	1,257,616

Page 32

1.	16	30	0	63	18	32	9	24
2.	8	14	1	0	6	6	10	36
3.	42	2	7	0	28	12	35	45
4.	3	30	8	54	14	10	20	18
5.	28	24	56	16	9	2	45	42
6.	18	56	24	36	5	0	32	42
7.	21	24	72	27	9	40	35	12
8.	40	9	12	72	32	8	16	24
9.	48	9	0	12	45	20	72	12
10.	49	15	4	8	28	14	27	0

Page 33

1.	162	210	343	95	148	624
2.	124	810	68	37	180	126
3.	60	272	333	26	125	511
4.	144	0	320	324	49	172
5.	108	0	186	136	324	770
6.	609	0	488	432	348	10
7.	504	828	225	124	630	138
8.	250	23	82	231	102	0

Page 34

1.	348	649	5,484	4,315	1,434	2,464
2.	2,528	2,994	3,357	2,922	6,125	4,040
3.	1,614	1,996	3,600	2,120	1,953	1,203
4.	2,448	1,718	3,856	4,590	772	1,584
5.	4,886	2,322	1,195	766	3,177	0
6.	1,656	558	6,657	1,233	2,832	1,650
7.	338	5,262	588	4,635	2,540	171

Page 35

1.	3,157	2,673	1,848	2,418	6,880	890
2.	871	4,671	4,980	1,068	1,048	1,440
3.	3,458	828	8,847	551	3,372	744
4.	2,216	1,995	206	6,636	608	1,308
5.	3,450	3,936	8,001	5,070	564	467
6.	1,115	1,860	750	3,672	1,364	2,637
7.	4,090	960	3,087	2,752	2,076	1,140
8.	4,085	504	6,853	4,851	1,460	1,504
9.	1,805	2,261	2,802	828	1,638	0

Page 36

1.	6,162	1,122	1,675	6,486	2,940	1,798
2.	2,115	1,760	989	2,208	2,166	5,742
3.	3,290	3,104	5,060	3,519	4,455	1,586
4.	3,168	1,314	1,034	4,900	1,312	2,200
5.	551	1,242	1,980	7,332	4,794	1,881
6.	3,750	945	4,599	770	9,506	6,020

Page 37

1.	3,180	1,800	840	2,548	1,071	6,804
2.	1,152	5,040	1,782	660	980	2,352
3.	2,646	3,094	4,674	2,592	3,731	418
4.	2,844	198	3,240	780	1,950	2,848
5.	5,544	4,757	4,067	3,588	495	1,562
6.	8,184	2,450	480	700	1,650	1,160

Page 38

1.	64,588	10,833	10,720	8,928	18,262	5,180
2.	23,760	7,956	13,962	9,243	25,376	18,391
3.	21,009	29,700	13,110	17,346	20,544	6,474
4.	10,188	51,996;	6,000	58,644	66,240	14,355

Page 39

1.	12,702	88,443	65,016	10,856	11,454	27,200
2.	13,288	11,480	39,591	52,886	81,984	33,210
3.	48,111	8,732	4,686	56,334	8,338	2,304
4.	52,383	11,250	24,119	67,396	31,344	39,204
5.	44,370	43,215	34,656	71,079	9,984	18,936
6.	17,856	38,076	64,989	12,304	11,880	10,212

Page 40

1.	816,775	481,500	593,568	96,712
2.	858,364	108,934	130,442	355,008
3.	1,992,711	2,784,960	1,660,811	1,112,034
4.	474,700	1,269,576	2,057,096	4,772,236

Page 41

1.	494,649	739,404	74,970	104,667
2.	210,962	331,890	66,861	23,316
3.	987,392	2,951,225	3,043,202	1,159,234
4.	637,186	986,225	2,406,144	3,563,604
5.	1,032,536	8,012,790	624,150	1,929,208

© RBP Books   www.summerbridgeactivities.com   Math Connection—Grade 5—RBP0172

Answer Pages

Page 42
1.	56	20	180	376
2.	0	910	3,024	4,310
3.	304	540	1,116	3,071
4.	2,250	2,790	1,209	1,204
5.	289,456	110,682	309,600	203,763
6.	2,714,250	1,769,526	5,940,768	1,923,316

Page 43
1. $24 **2.** $22 **3. a.** 4 pounds **b.** $28
4. $325 **5.** $186 **6.** 675 people

Page 44
1. 46 hours **2.** 75 hours **3.** 884 hours
4. 212 hours **5. a.** 1,217 total hours **b.** yes

Page 45
1.	45	21	344	304
2.	1,872	4,753	2,162	280
3.	46,458	22,589	39,196	19,448
4.	175,348	226,576	765,440	117,348
5.	2,328,651	6,203,709	2,392,677	1,681,688

Page 46
1. 128 **2.** 19 **3.** 30 **4.** 126
5. 14 **6.** 26 **7.** 11 **8.** 42

Page 47
1.	24	5R4	78R4	69R1
2.	602	620	4R3	4R6
3.	2R29	3R11	3R18	9R45
4.	23R8	8R1	37R53	100R12
5.	98R5	100R38	1,879R5	634R26

Page 48
1.	7	9	4	3	1	2
2.	2	3	7	9	6	3
3.	9	6	4	8	1	5
4.	9	0	8	4	8	2
5.	2	7	0	2	7	1
6.	5	2	0	1	7	2

Page 49
1.	16	12	23	19	33
2.	19	11	18	12	14
3.	13	8	29	30	21
4.	15	6	18	12	17
5.	12	4	66	13	11

Page 50
1.	120	160	28	34	282
2.	18	38	216	51	16
3.	112	27	154	234	102
4.	45	105	96	264	122

Page 51
1.	11R3	13R1	1R7	28R1	26
2.	95R2	55R3	119R2	286	241
3.	195R2	58	107	555	122R1
4.	247	31R2	62R1	105R6	130R4

Page 52
1.	1,628R5	533R3	804R1	900R1	1,007R1
2.	552	1,617R3	1,906R2	471R4	1,540
3.	556R2	1563	520	4,416	718R1
4.	448R1	602R4	131R4	468R1	752R1

Page 53
1.	31R4	20R1	207R3
2.	84R6	166	111R2
3.	1,096	4,642	969R4
4.	264R3	153	372

Page 54
1.	2R12	2R1	1R6	2R10	1R16
2.	2	1R8	1R10	1R1	1
3.	3R10	4	1R1	1R8	2R8
4.	2R6	1R7	2R5	1R2	3R10

Page 55
1.	1R79	40	16	4R30	2R26
2.	54	41	7R3	7R78	4R9
3.	4R9	6R54	3R31	8R23	1R64

Page 56
1.	9R27	31	4R22
2.	7R2	1R61	7R82
3.	16R8	35R12	5R54

Page 57
1.	13R78	52R1	92R92	46
2.	83R9	69R11	91R59	79
3.	55R26	262R6	91R29	161R41
4.	72	42R40	70R36	55

Page 58
1.	110R2	55	68R48	67R2
2.	52R16	59R1	120R1	420R7
3.	50	71R10	400R4	46
4.	16R5	84R27	51	35
5.	126R30	103R22	32R38	92
6.	132R9	22R2	65	25R25

Page 59
1.	238R26	733R6	537R42	533R33
2.	696R18	596R9	792R12	734R48
3.	1,001R28	970R20	850R15	2,280R14

Math Connection—Grade 5—RBP0172   www.summerbridgeactivities.com   ©RBP Books

Page 60
1. 222R5   140R30   120R20
2. 282R19   25R25   537R33
3. 544R17   882R40   211R51

Page 61
1. 13 human years
2. 8 human years
3. **a.** 7 years **b.** remainder 3
4. **a.** 8 years **b.** remainder 8
5. **a.** 29 years old **b.** 179 days

Page 62
1. 61 lawns   2. 250 square feet   3. $13 per lawn
4. $2   5. 144 hours   6. 12 hours

Page 63
1.   31   19R2   62R3   137R2
2. 1,472R2   905R3   3R9   6R2
3.   2R7   3   3   12R9
4.   17R22   8R18   90R77   156R3
5.   63R40   86R70   223R29   2,119R6

Page 64
1. 3 ft.   2. 68 in.   3. 8 in.
4. 2 mi.   5. 5 yd.   6. 5; 60
7. 6; 14   8. 10,560; 6   9. 20; 34
10. 87; 3   11. 31; 16,150   12. 7; 158
13. 26,543; 69

Page 65
1. 2 cups   2. 60 gal.   3. 2 gal.
4. 2 qt.   5. 10; 2   6. 4; 2
7. 12; 4   8. 88; 9   9. 9; 4
10. 11; 24   11. 11; 135   12. 29; 10

Page 66
1. 2 cups   2. 60 gal.   3. 2 gal.
1. 3 quarts   2. 10 ounces   3. 2 cups
4. 5,530 feet   5. 300 feet
6. **a.** 8 quarts **b.** Lorenzo **c.** 2 quarts
7. **a.** 24 inches **b.** 4 inches
8. 12 people

Page 67
1. $\frac{3}{8}$ $\frac{3}{4}$ $\frac{1}{2}$ $\frac{1}{6}$
2. $2\frac{2}{3}$ $1\frac{2}{5}$ $4\frac{1}{2}$
3. $1\frac{1}{4}$ $3\frac{1}{7}$ $1\frac{1}{2}$
4. $\frac{2}{3}$ $\frac{1}{3}$ $\frac{2}{9}$
5. $1\frac{1}{4}$ $4\frac{1}{2}$ $8\frac{2}{3}$
6.   12   14   3

Page 68
1. $\frac{3}{8}$ $\frac{5}{8}$ $\frac{4}{6}$ $\frac{2}{6}$ $\frac{4}{8}$ $\frac{4}{8}$ $\frac{5}{6}$ $\frac{1}{6}$
2. $\frac{1}{4}$ $\frac{3}{4}$ $\frac{2}{3}$ $\frac{1}{3}$ $\frac{1}{8}$ $\frac{7}{8}$ $\frac{6}{8}$ $\frac{2}{8}$
3. $\frac{1}{2}$ $\frac{1}{2}$ $\frac{1}{3}$ $\frac{2}{3}$ $\frac{2}{3}$ $\frac{1}{3}$ $\frac{2}{4}$ $\frac{2}{4}$
4. $\frac{3}{6}$ $\frac{3}{6}$ $\frac{1}{6}$ $\frac{5}{6}$ $\frac{2}{6}$ $\frac{4}{6}$ $\frac{4}{12}$ $\frac{8}{12}$

Page 69
1.

2.

3.

4.

5.

6.

Page 70
1. $\frac{3}{5}$; $\frac{3}{4}$ 2. $\frac{4}{9}$; $\frac{1}{4}$ 3. $\frac{1}{3}$; $\frac{6}{12}$
4. $\frac{2}{8}$; $\frac{4}{10}$ 5. $\frac{4}{5}$; $\frac{5}{11}$ 6. $\frac{1}{2}$; $\frac{7}{8}$
7. one-third   two-thirds
8. one-half   one-eighth
9. three-eighths   four-elevenths
10. two-fifths   five-thirds
11. five-sevenths   five-ninths
12. four-thirds   nine-halves

Page 71
1. $7\frac{1}{2}$ $1\frac{3}{4}$ $2\frac{6}{7}$
2. $8\frac{3}{5}$ $2\frac{7}{8}$ $4\frac{1}{5}$
3. $2\frac{7}{12}$ $2\frac{1}{2}$ $1\frac{5}{8}$
4. $2\frac{3}{4}$ $5\frac{4}{9}$ $6\frac{5}{6}$
5. $7\frac{2}{3}$ $11\frac{1}{4}$ $1\frac{3}{4}$
6. $3\frac{2}{7}$ 9   8

© RBP Books   www.summerbridgeactivities.com   Math Connection—Grade 5—RBP0172

Page 72

1. $1\frac{1}{4}$ $3\frac{1}{2}$ $1\frac{1}{5}$
2. $2\frac{2}{3}$ $4\frac{1}{2}$ $2\frac{2}{5}$
3. $1\frac{4}{5}$ $8\frac{6}{7}$ $4\frac{2}{3}$
4. $2\frac{2}{5}$ 8 $7\frac{5}{12}$
5. $3\frac{1}{3}$ $7\frac{8}{9}$ $10\frac{1}{6}$
6. $6\frac{1}{2}$ $10\frac{4}{5}$ $1\frac{2}{7}$
7. $4\frac{1}{12}$ 10 12
8. $3\frac{11}{12}$ 12 $9\frac{7}{10}$

Page 73

1. $\frac{7}{3}$ $\frac{27}{4}$ $\frac{13}{12}$
2. $\frac{25}{8}$ $\frac{38}{5}$ $\frac{19}{10}$
3. $\frac{17}{5}$ $\frac{103}{11}$ $\frac{27}{7}$
4. $\frac{25}{9}$ $\frac{53}{12}$ $\frac{73}{11}$

Page 74

1. $\frac{19}{5}$ $\frac{19}{8}$ $\frac{17}{12}$
2. $\frac{21}{8}$ $\frac{23}{4}$ $\frac{73}{9}$
3. $\frac{14}{3}$ $\frac{13}{2}$ $\frac{119}{3}$
4. $\frac{57}{8}$ $\frac{12}{7}$ $\frac{52}{11}$
5. $\frac{45}{7}$ $\frac{17}{5}$ $\frac{95}{12}$
6. $\frac{55}{8}$ $\frac{31}{12}$ $\frac{53}{10}$

Page 75

1. $\frac{1}{2}$ $\frac{2}{5}$ $\frac{1}{3}$
2. $\frac{2}{3}$ $\frac{1}{3}$ $\frac{3}{5}$
3. $\frac{3}{4}$ $\frac{1}{12}$ $\frac{2}{3}$
4. $\frac{1}{3}$ $\frac{1}{4}$ $\frac{5}{6}$
5. $\frac{1}{2}$ $\frac{1}{4}$ 1

Page 76

1. $\frac{1}{2}$ $\frac{5}{6}$ $\frac{1}{3}$
2. $\frac{5}{12}$ $\frac{1}{12}$ $\frac{2}{3}$
3. $\frac{2}{7}$ $\frac{1}{9}$ $\frac{1}{3}$
4. $\frac{1}{2}$ 1 $\frac{1}{3}$
5. $\frac{1}{3}$ $\frac{3}{5}$ $\frac{1}{2}$
6. $\frac{1}{3}$ $\frac{3}{4}$ $\frac{1}{8}$
7. $\frac{2}{3}$ $\frac{7}{20}$ $\frac{1}{2}$
8. $\frac{2}{5}$ $\frac{1}{3}$ $\frac{2}{3}$

Page 77

1. $2\frac{1}{2}$ $3\frac{1}{3}$ $2\frac{3}{4}$
2. $1\frac{2}{3}$ $6\frac{1}{2}$ 7
3. $2\frac{1}{4}$ $4\frac{1}{3}$ $6\frac{1}{2}$
4. 7 $5\frac{1}{4}$ $3\frac{1}{2}$

Page 78

1. $\frac{1}{3}$ $\frac{2}{3}$ $\frac{5}{6}$
2. $\frac{3}{4}$ $\frac{1}{6}$ $\frac{1}{2}$
3. $1\frac{1}{8}$ $2\frac{1}{5}$ $2\frac{2}{3}$
4. $5\frac{1}{3}$ $1\frac{1}{2}$ $4\frac{1}{2}$
5. $1\frac{1}{3}$ $2\frac{2}{3}$ $4\frac{1}{4}$
6. $6\frac{1}{3}$ $4\frac{3}{4}$ $7\frac{1}{2}$

Page 79

1. 9 12 4
2. 4 15 12
3. 15 4 10

Page 80

1. 4 20 15
2. 9 10 44
3. 3 36 10
4. 5 6 12

Page 81

1. $\frac{10}{15}, \frac{12}{15}$ $\frac{3}{6}, \frac{2}{6}$ $\frac{4}{10}, \frac{5}{10}$
2. $\frac{15}{20}, \frac{4}{20}$ $\frac{3}{21}, \frac{14}{21}$ $\frac{18}{21}, \frac{7}{21}$
3. $\frac{5}{10}, \frac{6}{10}$ $\frac{8}{14}, \frac{7}{14}$ $\frac{16}{24}, \frac{15}{24}$

Page 82

1. $\frac{4}{6}, \frac{5}{6}$ $\frac{2}{4}, \frac{1}{4}$ $\frac{4}{10}, \frac{1}{10}$
2. $\frac{9}{12}, \frac{1}{12}$ $\frac{2}{14}, \frac{2}{14}$ $\frac{6}{9}, \frac{3}{9}$
3. $\frac{1}{10}, \frac{6}{10}$ $\frac{3}{8}, \frac{4}{8}$ $\frac{6}{8}, \frac{5}{8}$

Page 83

1. $\frac{4}{24}, \frac{15}{24}$ $\frac{3}{12}, \frac{2}{12}$ $\frac{6}{18}, \frac{1}{18}$
2. $\frac{15}{20}, \frac{2}{20}$ $\frac{3}{24}, \frac{4}{24}$ $\frac{8}{12}, \frac{1}{12}$
3. $\frac{21}{30}, \frac{15}{30}$ $\frac{15}{40}, \frac{4}{40}$ $\frac{9}{12}, \frac{10}{12}$

Page 84

1. 2 **2.** $\frac{1}{4}$ cup   **3.** $2\frac{1}{2}$ teaspoons

4. $7\frac{1}{2}$ cups   **5.** $2\frac{1}{2}$ cups   **6.** coconut

Answer Pages

Page 85

1. $2\frac{1}{3}$ $2\frac{1}{5}$ $2\frac{1}{2}$ $1\frac{1}{8}$
2. $\frac{8}{5}$ $\frac{14}{3}$ $\frac{31}{6}$ $\frac{29}{8}$
3. $\frac{3}{4}$ $\frac{1}{3}$ $\frac{1}{8}$ $\frac{3}{10}$
4. $2\frac{3}{4}$ $3\frac{3}{4}$ $6\frac{1}{3}$ $1\frac{2}{5}$
5.   3   16   20   6

Page 86

1. 11 m; 1 cm   2. 1 m; 18 cm   3. 28 cm; 2 m
4. 1 mm; 350,000 km   5. m
6. km   7. cm   9. mm
10. m   11. cm

Page 87

1. 4,200; 62   2. 4,000; 8   3. 850; 540
4. >; (bigger than 1 meter)   5. yes
6. 500 cm   7. 35 km

Page 88

1. 3.8 l; 5 ml   2. 1 kl; 1 ml   3. 2,000; 2
4. 5,000; 45   5. 24,000; 38,000
6. 2,000 ml; 8 servings

Page 89

1. 5 kg; 6 g   2. $3\frac{1}{2}$ kg; 34 kg   3. 7,000; 6
4. 12,000; 73   5. 2,000 grams   6. 250 grams
8. 3 slices

Page 90

1. 7 cm   2. 9 cm   3. 3 cm
4. 15 cm   5. 65 mm   6. 56 mm
7. 104 mm   8-10. Check answers.

Page 91

1. 14 cm; 16 cm   2. 12 cm; 9 cm
3. 120 mm; 116 mm

Page 92

1. 12 yd.; 12 ft.
2. 14 ft.; 12 yd.
3. 35 in.; 22 ft.
4. 10 yd.; 30 in.

Page 93

1. 12; 25   2. 20; 84   3. 18   4. 4
5. 30   6. 15   7. 5

Page 94

1. $\frac{4}{5}$ $\frac{1}{2}$ $1\frac{3}{5}$ 1
2. $3\frac{1}{2}$ $5\frac{2}{3}$ $16\frac{2}{7}$ 13
3. $\frac{11}{12}$ $1\frac{7}{12}$ $11\frac{1}{6}$ $6\frac{3}{10}$

4. $\frac{3}{4}$ $1\frac{3}{5}$ $\frac{1}{2}$ $1\frac{5}{6}$
5. $\frac{1}{12}$ $\frac{11}{24}$ $5\frac{2}{7}$ $4\frac{13}{15}$

Page 95

1. $\frac{1}{2}$ 2. $\frac{1}{4}$; $\frac{3}{4}$ 3. $\frac{3}{8}$; $\frac{5}{8}$ 4. $\frac{1}{6}$; $\frac{4}{6}$

Page 96

1. $\frac{4}{5}$ $\frac{2}{3}$ $\frac{2}{3}$ $\frac{1}{3}$
2. $\frac{3}{7}$ $\frac{1}{2}$ $\frac{5}{12}$ $\frac{7}{10}$
3. $\frac{5}{6}$ $\frac{4}{11}$ $\frac{3}{4}$ $\frac{7}{9}$
4. $\frac{4}{9}$ $\frac{2}{3}$ $\frac{7}{11}$ $\frac{7}{8}$

Page 97

1.   1 $1\frac{1}{3}$ $1\frac{1}{7}$ $\frac{1}{2}$
2. $1\frac{1}{5}$ $\frac{1}{2}$ 1 $1\frac{1}{2}$
3. $1\frac{2}{7}$ $\frac{5}{8}$ $1\frac{2}{3}$ $\frac{2}{3}$
4. $1\frac{1}{5}$ $1\frac{1}{2}$ $1\frac{1}{4}$ $1\frac{1}{3}$

Page 98

1. $5\frac{2}{3}$ $4\frac{3}{5}$ 6 $13\frac{1}{2}$
2. $6\frac{1}{5}$ $14\frac{1}{2}$ $4\frac{1}{2}$ $6\frac{3}{7}$
3.   13 $6\frac{1}{3}$ $4\frac{1}{10}$ $4\frac{4}{5}$
4. $5\frac{3}{4}$ $8\frac{1}{3}$ $18\frac{1}{3}$ $41\frac{1}{10}$

Page 99

1. $\frac{11}{15}$ $\frac{17}{24}$ $\frac{5}{6}$ $1\frac{7}{20}$
2. $1\frac{7}{30}$ $\frac{20}{21}$ $\frac{19}{30}$ $1\frac{1}{18}$
3. $\frac{25}{28}$ $\frac{23}{24}$ $1\frac{1}{12}$ $1\frac{11}{30}$

Page 100

1. $1\frac{1}{9}$ $\frac{7}{8}$ $\frac{7}{10}$ $1\frac{1}{8}$
2. $1\frac{1}{6}$ $\frac{7}{15}$ $\frac{5}{6}$ $1\frac{5}{8}$
3. $1\frac{3}{8}$ $\frac{7}{8}$ $\frac{13}{14}$ $1\frac{1}{4}$

Page 101

1. $\frac{5}{12}$ $\frac{19}{24}$ $1\frac{7}{12}$ $\frac{13}{15}$
2. $1\frac{2}{9}$ $\frac{7}{15}$ $1\frac{1}{20}$ $1\frac{17}{24}$
3. $1\frac{2}{15}$ $\frac{11}{18}$ $\frac{19}{24}$ $1\frac{21}{40}$

Page 102

1. $5\frac{13}{24}$ $5\frac{19}{20}$ $7\frac{1}{6}$ $5\frac{11}{12}$
2. $7\frac{1}{4}$ $7\frac{11}{15}$ $6\frac{11}{12}$ $4\frac{1}{24}$
3. $7\frac{1}{4}$ $5\frac{1}{10}$ $9\frac{7}{8}$ $12\frac{3}{22}$

© RBP Books   www.summerbridgeactivities.com   Math Connection—Grade 5—RBP0172

Answer Pages

Page 103
1. $\frac{1}{2}$ $\frac{1}{2}$ $\frac{2}{5}$ $1\frac{1}{3}$
2. $2\frac{2}{3}$ 9 3 $9\frac{1}{3}$
3. $3\frac{2}{7}$ $5\frac{1}{7}$ $5\frac{9}{11}$ $1\frac{1}{6}$
4. $1\frac{11}{24}$ $\frac{19}{20}$ $\frac{3}{5}$ $\frac{13}{24}$
5. $8\frac{1}{6}$ $7\frac{11}{24}$ $6\frac{5}{18}$ $4\frac{1}{2}$

Page 104
1. $\frac{1}{4}$ $\frac{1}{6}$ $\frac{2}{3}$ $\frac{3}{7}$
2. $\frac{5}{6}$ $\frac{3}{5}$ $\frac{2}{5}$ $\frac{1}{3}$
3. $\frac{1}{2}$ $\frac{1}{2}$ $\frac{7}{11}$ $\frac{5}{8}$

Page 105
1. $4\frac{1}{8}$ $2\frac{2}{3}$ $5\frac{2}{9}$ $3\frac{3}{5}$
2. $7\frac{1}{5}$ $4\frac{5}{9}$ $11\frac{8}{11}$ $8\frac{1}{9}$
3. $6\frac{2}{3}$ $9\frac{4}{5}$ $11\frac{3}{10}$ $7\frac{1}{6}$

Page 106
1. $1\frac{5}{7}$ $2\frac{2}{3}$ $\frac{1}{3}$ $5\frac{3}{4}$
2. $2\frac{3}{5}$ $\frac{3}{5}$ $2\frac{3}{5}$ $2\frac{5}{6}$
3. $\frac{1}{2}$ $\frac{2}{3}$ $1\frac{5}{6}$ $5\frac{1}{2}$

Page 107
1. $2\frac{1}{2}$ $1\frac{6}{7}$ $\frac{1}{2}$ $1\frac{3}{4}$
2. $\frac{2}{7}$ $2\frac{3}{5}$ $3\frac{3}{5}$ $3\frac{1}{3}$
3. $1\frac{9}{11}$ $\frac{2}{3}$ $2\frac{4}{5}$ $\frac{1}{2}$
4. $4\frac{1}{2}$ $5\frac{5}{7}$ $4\frac{1}{2}$ $9\frac{2}{3}$
5. $\frac{1}{4}$ $4\frac{3}{5}$ $2\frac{1}{4}$ $7\frac{1}{3}$

Page 108
1. $\frac{5}{12}$ $\frac{3}{10}$ $\frac{1}{6}$ $\frac{3}{14}$
2. $\frac{5}{18}$ $\frac{8}{21}$ $\frac{11}{20}$ $\frac{18}{35}$
3. $\frac{17}{45}$ $\frac{19}{40}$ $\frac{29}{42}$ $\frac{43}{66}$

Page 109
1. $\frac{1}{20}$ $\frac{11}{18}$ $\frac{1}{8}$ $\frac{4}{9}$
2. $\frac{1}{3}$ $\frac{1}{5}$ $\frac{3}{8}$ $\frac{1}{10}$
3. $\frac{11}{24}$ $\frac{8}{15}$ $\frac{7}{12}$ $\frac{1}{24}$

Page 110
1. $\frac{1}{6}$ $\frac{19}{30}$ $\frac{7}{12}$ $\frac{1}{10}$
2. $\frac{3}{8}$ $\frac{1}{5}$ $\frac{1}{4}$ $\frac{3}{8}$
3. $\frac{7}{24}$ $\frac{1}{2}$ $\frac{4}{9}$ $\frac{7}{18}$
4. $\frac{11}{24}$ $\frac{1}{6}$ $\frac{5}{12}$ $\frac{1}{3}$
5. $\frac{1}{2}$ $\frac{7}{20}$ $\frac{1}{12}$ $\frac{2}{15}$

Page 111
1. $1\frac{5}{6}$ $\frac{23}{24}$ $1\frac{3}{4}$ $3\frac{4}{15}$
2. $\frac{5}{8}$ $\frac{5}{9}$ $1\frac{5}{6}$ $1\frac{7}{10}$
3. $1\frac{17}{24}$ $3\frac{3}{8}$ $3\frac{1}{2}$ $\frac{3}{4}$

Page 112
1. $\frac{1}{2}$ $\frac{4}{21}$ $2\frac{2}{3}$ $5\frac{1}{8}$
2. $\frac{3}{10}$ $\frac{1}{8}$ $2\frac{1}{2}$ $7\frac{1}{2}$
3. $\frac{1}{3}$ $6\frac{1}{2}$ $6\frac{5}{12}$ $1\frac{8}{15}$
4. $9\frac{2}{5}$ 4 $\frac{10}{33}$ $\frac{7}{24}$
5. 9 $\frac{1}{6}$ $1\frac{1}{6}$ $\frac{5}{8}$

Page 113
1. $2\frac{1}{3}$ $\frac{1}{8}$ $4\frac{1}{24}$ $\frac{1}{3}$
2. $3\frac{3}{14}$ $\frac{1}{6}$ $\frac{1}{2}$ $\frac{5}{24}$
3. $6\frac{3}{8}$ $3\frac{14}{15}$ $2\frac{1}{24}$ $\frac{5}{12}$
4. $3\frac{1}{6}$ $\frac{4}{11}$ $5\frac{2}{3}$ $2\frac{9}{10}$
5. $\frac{1}{4}$ $3\frac{4}{9}$ $\frac{17}{24}$ $6\frac{5}{12}$

Page 114
1. $\frac{5}{12}$ mile   2. **a.** $\frac{11}{12}$ mile   **b.** $\frac{1}{12}$ mile
3. **a.** $\frac{3}{4}$ mile **b.** $\frac{1}{4}$ mile   4. $6\frac{1}{3}$ minutes

Page 115
1. $3\frac{11}{12}$ hours   2. $\frac{7}{12}$ hour   3. $\frac{2}{3}$ hour
4. $2\frac{5}{12}$ hours   5. $1\frac{1}{12}$ hours   6. Tyrell

Page 116
1. $\frac{4}{7}$ 1 $\frac{2}{3}$ $1\frac{2}{3}$
2. $3\frac{2}{5}$ 9 11 $4\frac{1}{2}$
3. $\frac{19}{24}$ $\frac{11}{12}$ $11\frac{5}{6}$ $6\frac{2}{15}$
4. $\frac{1}{2}$ $3\frac{2}{5}$ $1\frac{1}{2}$ $3\frac{2}{3}$
5. $\frac{1}{2}$ $\frac{1}{12}$ $6\frac{4}{7}$ $12\frac{1}{3}$

Page 117
1. certain   2. impossible   3. likely
4. unlikely   5. unlikely

Page 118
1. $\frac{1}{5}$ 2. $\frac{2}{5}$ 3. 0
4. 0   5. 1   6. $\frac{2}{5}$

Page 119
1. $\frac{4}{15}$ 2. $\frac{1}{5}$ 3. 0   4. $\frac{7}{15}$
5. $\frac{1}{3}$ 6. 1   7. $\frac{2}{5}$ 8. $\frac{3}{5}$

Math Connection—Grade 5—RBP0172   www.summerbridgeactivities.com   © RBP Books

Answer Pages

Page 120

1. $\frac{2}{21}$ $\frac{3}{20}$ $\frac{4}{15}$ $\frac{8}{33}$
2. $\frac{12}{21}$ $\frac{6}{22}$ $\frac{10}{21}$ $\frac{5}{12}$
3. $1\frac{1}{3}$ $5\frac{1}{4}$ $1\frac{4}{5}$ $1\frac{11}{24}$
4. $1\frac{1}{5}$ $\frac{8}{15}$ $\frac{5}{6}$ $1\frac{1}{8}$
5. 7 $7\frac{1}{2}$ 10 $1\frac{2}{3}$
6. $4\frac{1}{12}$ 4 $8\frac{2}{5}$ $7\frac{11}{30}$

Page 121

1. $\frac{2}{15}$ 2. $\frac{1}{12}$ 3. $\frac{1}{4}$ 4. $\frac{3}{8}$ 5. $\frac{3}{10}$ 6. $\frac{1}{6}$

Page 122

1. $\frac{3}{8}$ $\frac{2}{15}$ $\frac{2}{15}$ $\frac{5}{12}$
2. $\frac{3}{32}$ $\frac{5}{24}$ $\frac{5}{14}$ $\frac{1}{12}$
3. $\frac{2}{25}$ $\frac{3}{10}$ $\frac{9}{20}$ $\frac{3}{32}$
4. $\frac{6}{25}$ $\frac{1}{4}$ $\frac{4}{9}$ $\frac{3}{16}$
5. $\frac{5}{21}$ $\frac{3}{14}$ $\frac{5}{24}$ $\frac{5}{18}$
6. $\frac{3}{35}$ $\frac{1}{16}$ $\frac{3}{28}$ $\frac{5}{18}$

Page 123

1. $\frac{1}{4}$ $\frac{2}{5}$ $\frac{2}{7}$ $\frac{2}{7}$
2. $\frac{5}{9}$ $\frac{1}{10}$ $\frac{1}{3}$ $\frac{1}{4}$
3. $\frac{1}{16}$ $\frac{4}{7}$ $\frac{1}{12}$ $\frac{1}{6}$
4. $\frac{3}{16}$ $\frac{2}{15}$ $\frac{2}{7}$ $\frac{1}{6}$
5. $\frac{1}{7}$ $\frac{1}{4}$ $\frac{1}{3}$ $\frac{1}{5}$

Page 124

1. $\frac{1}{16}$ $\frac{1}{5}$ $\frac{3}{7}$ $\frac{1}{7}$
2. $\frac{2}{11}$ $\frac{5}{16}$ $\frac{1}{6}$ $\frac{1}{3}$
3. $\frac{2}{27}$ $\frac{1}{7}$ $\frac{1}{4}$ $\frac{10}{27}$
4. $\frac{4}{7}$ $\frac{1}{10}$ $\frac{3}{5}$ $\frac{1}{5}$
5. $\frac{1}{6}$ $\frac{2}{3}$ $\frac{1}{4}$ $\frac{5}{8}$
6. $\frac{1}{3}$ $\frac{11}{14}$ $\frac{3}{14}$ $\frac{1}{8}$

Page 125

1. 2 $1\frac{3}{5}$ $\frac{6}{7}$ $1\frac{1}{7}$
2. $2\frac{2}{5}$ $\frac{9}{10}$ $6\frac{3}{4}$ $1\frac{4}{5}$
3. $1\frac{1}{3}$ $1\frac{5}{7}$ $\frac{3}{5}$ $1\frac{1}{2}$
4. $1\frac{1}{2}$ $1\frac{1}{9}$ $\frac{6}{7}$ $2\frac{2}{3}$

Page 126

1. $\frac{9}{16}$ $\frac{7}{9}$ $1\frac{1}{2}$ $1\frac{1}{7}$
2. $\frac{7}{8}$ $2\frac{1}{10}$ $1\frac{1}{3}$ $3\frac{1}{2}$
3. $1\frac{7}{12}$ $\frac{5}{18}$ $\frac{4}{5}$ $\frac{5}{9}$
4. $3\frac{1}{2}$ $1\frac{7}{12}$ $1\frac{9}{16}$ $\frac{7}{8}$

Page 127

1. $6\frac{1}{2}$ $3\frac{3}{5}$ $3\frac{6}{7}$ $9\frac{1}{7}$
2. $6\frac{4}{5}$ $6\frac{9}{10}$ $15\frac{3}{4}$ $12\frac{9}{10}$
3. $12\frac{1}{2}$ $7\frac{5}{7}$ $12\frac{3}{5}$ $21\frac{1}{2}$
4. $9\frac{1}{5}$ $12\frac{7}{9}$ $10\frac{2}{7}$ $26\frac{2}{3}$

Page 128

1. 10 $3\frac{1}{8}$ $4\frac{19}{20}$ $2\frac{3}{5}$
2. $2\frac{6}{25}$ $8\frac{1}{3}$ $7\frac{1}{2}$ $14\frac{7}{10}$
3. $5\frac{13}{24}$ $2\frac{1}{4}$ $1\frac{27}{28}$ $5\frac{1}{2}$
4. $6\frac{3}{10}$ $5\frac{1}{2}$ $6\frac{3}{4}$ $7\frac{45}{56}$

Page 129

1. $\frac{3}{8}$ $\frac{2}{15}$ $\frac{4}{15}$ $\frac{15}{32}$
2. $\frac{2}{5}$ $\frac{4}{9}$ $\frac{3}{10}$ $\frac{2}{11}$
3. 2 $2\frac{1}{2}$ $5\frac{1}{3}$ $5\frac{3}{5}$
4. 1 $\frac{3}{5}$ $\frac{3}{4}$ $1\frac{7}{8}$
5. $13\frac{3}{4}$ 3 11 $5\frac{1}{3}$
6. $4\frac{1}{12}$ $3\frac{3}{4}$ $2\frac{13}{16}$ $3\frac{1}{30}$

Page 130

1. $2\frac{2}{5}$ miles 2. $\frac{3}{5}$ gallon 3. $4.00
4. $\frac{1}{4}$ barrel 5. $\frac{3}{5}$ mile

Page 131

1. 3 students 2. 9 girls 3. 4 students
4. $\frac{3}{4}$ hour 5. $1\frac{1}{6}$ hours

Page 132

1. $\frac{2}{15}$ $\frac{5}{24}$ $\frac{5}{18}$ $\frac{7}{30}$
2. $\frac{2}{11}$ $\frac{3}{7}$ $\frac{1}{14}$ $\frac{3}{8}$
3. $1\frac{1}{3}$ 6 $1\frac{2}{3}$ 2
4. $1\frac{5}{7}$ $\frac{7}{8}$ $2\frac{1}{12}$ $1\frac{7}{8}$
5. $3\frac{2}{3}$ $6\frac{1}{4}$ $16\frac{1}{2}$ $6\frac{8}{9}$
6. $6\frac{5}{12}$ 2 $5\frac{2}{3}$ $3\frac{13}{24}$

Page 133

1. $\frac{7}{2}$ 4 $\frac{9}{2}$
2. $\frac{7}{4}$ 2 $\frac{9}{4}$
3. $\frac{1}{32}$ $\frac{1}{64}$ $\frac{1}{128}$
4. $4\frac{1}{3}$ 5 $5\frac{2}{3}$
5. $\frac{81}{5}$ $\frac{243}{5}$ $\frac{729}{5}$
6. $\frac{1}{3}$ $\frac{1}{2}$ 1
7. $\frac{1}{2}$ $\frac{1}{3}$ $\frac{1}{6}$
8. 6 $5\frac{1}{2}$ 5
9. 4 $3\frac{2}{3}$ $3\frac{1}{3}$
10. $\frac{6}{25}$ $\frac{7}{30}$ $\frac{8}{35}$

© RBP Books
www.summerbridgeactivities.com
Math Connection—Grade 5—RBP0172

Answer Pages

Page 134

1. $\frac{3}{10}$

2. one and twelve-hundredths; $1\frac{12}{100}$

3. .221; $\frac{221}{1000}$

4. .53; fifty-three hundredths

5. eight hundred seventy-one thousandths; $\frac{871}{1000}$

6. 2.01; two and one-hundredth

Page 135

1. 4.4; .23
2. 1.03; .5
3. .548; 2.53
4. 53.17; 16.303
5. .091; 91.3
6. $2\frac{87}{100}$; $\frac{983}{1000}$
7. $14\frac{5}{10}$; $287\frac{69}{100}$
8. $1\frac{752}{1000}$; $\frac{7}{10}$
9. $\frac{6}{100}$; $10\frac{54}{1000}$
10. $81\frac{2}{10}$; $\frac{157}{1000}$

Page 136

1. $\frac{2}{10}$; .2
2. $\frac{8}{10}$; .8
3. $\frac{9}{10}$; .9
4. $\frac{1}{10}$; .1
5. $\frac{13}{100}$; .13
6. $\frac{87}{100}$; .87
7. $\frac{55}{100}$; .55

Page 137

1. < 2. < 3. > 4. > 5. < 6. <
7. < 8. = 9. < 10. < 11. > 12. >
13. > 14. < 15. = 16. > 17. < 18. >

Page 138

Soda 1.05; Milk 1.07; Fries 1.10; Salad 1.25; Cheese Sandwich 2.03; Tuna Sandwich 2.15; Hamburger 2.21; Cheeseburger 2.51

1. 4.55
2. 10.75
3. 2.52
4. 1.847
5. 89.90

Page 139

1. line
2. ray
3. line segment
4. intersecting; parallel
5. intersecting; perpendicular

Page 140

1. acute; right
2. right; obtuse
3. obtuse; acute
4. obtuse; acute
5. right; acute

Page 141

1. pentagon; quadrilateral
2. triangle; heptagon
3. pentagon; octagon

Page 142

1. a, b, c, d; a, b, c
2. a, b;   a, b, c
3. a, b;   a, b, c, d, e

Page 143

1. congruent; similar
2. congruent; similar
3. similar; similar

Page 144

1. cylinder; rectangular prism
2. triangular prism; cone
3. pyramid; sphere

Page 145

1. 6   12
2. 5   9
3. 6   12
4. 8   18
5. 14 36

Page 146

1. 3   0   6
2. 4   3   1
3. 0   1   1
4. 2   4   5

Page 147

1.
2.
3.
4.
5.
6.

Page 148

1. 1,133 tickets
2. 14 songs
3. 16 minutes 39 seconds
4. $16,995
5. $7,875

Page 149

1. $\frac{1}{6}$
2. **a.** 12 points **b.** $\frac{1}{7}$
3. 60 minutes
4. 21 points
5. **a.** 4,200 square ft; 4,700 square ft. **b.** 500 square ft.

Page 150

1. 1,300 miles
2. 150 miles
3. $92
4. **a.** drive **b.** $832